The Marriage Journey

A Flight Plan to Your Healthy Marriage

Chuck and Mae Dettman

ISBN: 098389874X
ISBN-13: 978-0-9838987-4-0

Unless otherwise noted, all scripture verses used are from THE HOLY BIBLE, NEW INTERNATIONAL VERSION®, NIV® Copyright ©

1973, 1978, 1984, 2010 by Biblica, Inc. ™ Used by permission. All rights reserved worldwide.

Library of Congress Cataloging-in-Publication Data is on file at the Library of Congress, Washington, DC.

Scripture quotations marked (NLT) are taken from the Holy Bible, New Living Translation, copyright © 1996, 2004, 2007 by Tyndale House Foundation. Used by permission of Tyndale House Publishers, Inc., Carol Stream, Illinois 60188. All rights reserved.

ISBN 13: 978-0-9838987-4-0

1. Marriage-Religious aspects-Christianity. 2. Marriage-Biblical teaching. 3. Relationships. 4. Interpersonal relations–Religious aspects–Christianity. 5. Conflict management-Religious aspects-Christianity.

This book is available at large quantity discounts for use in denominational or regional marriage initiatives and can be customized with your organization or denomination's logo. For more information, contact **Sales@TheMarriage-Journey.com.**

Printed in the United States of America.

Acknowledgements

We are deeply grateful to those who have helped us throughout our 45 plus years of marriage and more than 25 years of marriage mentoring.

First, to our parents, for giving us the permission to "take-off" at the age of 19 on The Marriage Journey, even though they were convinced 'you'll never last past 6-months.'

Secondly, thanks to the many pastors we have proudly served with, enabling us to learn and gain so much knowledge. You provided opportunities for us to mentor couples and guide marriage ministries in your churches, avowed us by your advice and support, and invested in our development as mentors and leaders.

Third, a special thanks to our publisher, CreateSpace; our editor, Gregory S. Baker; our medical advisors, Celeste Li, M.D. and John Li, M.D.; and great friend David E Pennington for his injection of humor. You are all special partners in making our dream for this book become an actuality.

Our goal and prayer is for marriages to be blessed for generations to come as a result of the impact each of you have had on our lives.

Introduction

Welcome Aboard!

"Don't be afraid of them. Remember the Lord, who is great and awesome, and fight for your families, your sons and your daughters, your wives and your homes." (Nehemiah 4:14)

Nehemiah was assigned the task to rebuild a crumbling wall. He was desperate, saying *"... the city where my fathers are buried lies in ruins, and its gates have been destroyed by fire."* (Nehemiah 2:3) That's a remarkably accurate description of the American family today. Families destroyed by the epidemic of divorce; youth are increasingly exposed to unwholesome media to fuel the fire of premarital sex, drug abuse and suicide. The wall *(marriage and family unit)* is crumbling! The broken, crumbled wall can be restored, using the flight plans in *The Marriage Journey*.

We give attention to almost every element of our surroundings, (vehicles, homes, clothing, offices, body, and more) but neglect our marriages. Consider this, if you never change the oil in the vehicle, what happens? It breaks down and stops running. Neglect the home; it also becomes uninhabitable over time. We are bombarded with advertisements to support healthy lifestyles by Fitness Centers, Diet Programs, and Pharmaceuticals; all attempting to convince us we 'need their product to maintain health.' Do you ever see the same philosophy applied to our marriages? Left without maintenance, they too will become unhealthy. Not once have I seen an advertisement directed toward building a healthy, strong and lasting marriage on the evening news, during Prime Time TV or as a sponsor for a major sports event! Why? Most likely because we take marriage for granted; and no one has figured out how to profit from healthy marriages. There is more money to be made in divorces. Lawyers, accountants and auctioneers benefit from divorces. Nobody makes a dime if you are blissfully married.

Marriages and relationships are a lot like taking a flight across the country. Before you actually board your plane, no one knows how your flight will go! Not even the pilot! We all ASSUME it will be smooth flying, and take it for granted that we will land safely. Like any flight, marriages can start out smooth and turbulence-free, but sometimes, unexpected turbulence or challenges can happen at any time. It is important for you to remember, that if any turbulence or situation is encountered we all want to arrive at our destination.

God is the author of the ideal flight plan (the Bible). It is up to the co-pilots (husband and wife) to follow it. If they deviate, they wind up in trouble with the FAA; wander into bad weather, run out of gas, etc. You have no control over your destiny; it is all in the pilot's hands. Whereas God gives us free will so we CAN and DO deviate from his flight plan; He is the big eye in the sky. He is the Air Traffic Controller who can see where the other planes are, and where the storms are, and then vector you around them.

In order to board the plane, the crew must have many skills and lots of knowledge. The Captain completes his pre-flight checkup, files the flight plan, luggage is properly stowed, the weather is acceptable, and then the passengers are given the ok to board. Crews check and re-check the passenger comforts and safety. The take-off requires full throttle, (proper planning, preparation and maintenance), the right altitude, attitude and speed. Like most flights, we need navigation tools, safety practices and proper flight procedures for healthy marriages as well. One goal of *The Marriage Journey* is to provide "lift" for marriages to highest, safest and best "altitude" possible. We never anticipate a crash landing, but without careful guidance and control, the flight can become disastrous very quickly. We must seek God as the uplift and pilot, the key element in the flight. Skills in communication, conflict resolution, financial management, Biblical study and more are some of the gear to help maintain a great, thriving marriage (flight).

Chuck & Mae often open their mentoring sessions describing a marriage as similar to preparing for a long flight. The flight ought to have a mechanically sound aircraft, and 2 pilots (God plus the husband and wife co-pilots) cooperating with each other to follow the best flight plan laid out for them. They need to follow their checklists, practice emergency procedures and be prepared for the bad weather and emergencies Satan throws at them.

The purpose of *The Marriage Journey* is to share the flight patterns to create a strong, healthy and lasting marriage. (We like to call it the intercontinental flight.) It is designed for couples at any age or stage in their relationship. You can turn a good marriage into a great one, find hope in a struggling one, or take a great marriage to a deeper, more passionate level.

A great resource is our Navigational Cards. The Cards can be used, and serve, as Navigation "Check Points" similar to most flight requirements to report their route Check Points with flight control centers! Each day a new word is defined by its relativity to marriage. That word is intended to provoke discussion, thought and strength to the couple. The Navigation Cards help couples to learn where they are aligned and reveal strength in their marriage; yet other times they'll discover a word that prompts an opportunity for growth. (We call it flight path adjustment.) Together, the couple can experience joy and a better understanding of their spouse by using a simple set of cards (flight guides). (More on how to obtain and use the Navigation Cards is discussed in Chapter 18)

Welcome aboard! Sit back and enjoy your flight.

Recommended Resources

Olson, David H. L., and Amy K. Olson. *Empowering Couples: Building on Your Strengths*. Minneapolis, MN: Life Innovations, 2000.

Stoop, David A., and Jan Stoop. *The Complete Marriage Book: Collected Wisdom from Leading Marriage Experts*. Grand Rapids, MI: F.H. Revell, 2002.

CONTENTS

Additional resources, updates and downloadable material is available from www.themarriage-journey/resources

Marriage Leaders Comments

Chuck and Mae have written a great book to help your marriage soar long before you ever take off down the runway. In *The Marriage Journey*, you will be encouraged to do things God's way so you can experience the greatest joy in partnership and unity that you will have with another person. I know it will get you headed in the right direction on the path to a bright future together.

Dr. Tom Mullins
Founding Pastor, Christ Fellowship

"Travel with the Dettman's on *The Marriage Journey* and it will be an unforgettable trip. Using the analogy of plane travel the Dettman's used in the book, the *Journey* will help couples explore new territories and make surprising discoveries. To succeed, marriage requires clear flight plans to avoid thunder storms and have a smoother journey. Using navigation cards, couples can discover the best direction to fly and deal with unexpected turbulence. As pilot and co-pilot, couples need to work as a team to make the flight as enjoyable as possible for themselves and their passengers. The *Journey* will help couples have a pleasant trip and appreciate the beauty of the skies. Enjoy the flight!"

David H. Olson, Ph.D. *Professor Emeritus, University of Minnesota and Founder of PREPARE/ENRICH.*

The Marriage Journey gives helpful navigational aids you can easily apply during the stormy times of your marriage flight. The aeronautical theme gives an uplifting perspective to the turbulence often experienced in marriage. *The Journey* checkups, flight plans, and more, make for an easy read, plus offer a fresh and unclouded approach to help you build a strong marriage and family.

Claudia & David Arp, MSW
Speakers and authors of
10 Great Dates: Connecting Faith, Love & Marriage
(10Greatdates.org)

Chapter 01

Our Union with Christ
God Is the Pilot – We Are the Co-Pilots

The Apostle John writes, *"Dear friends, since God so loved us, we also ought to love one another. No one has ever seen God; but if we love one another, God lives in us and his love is made complete in us"* (1 John 4:11-12). In order to experience a true sense of closeness in marriage, it is vital that we understand the very heart of the gospel message: *we have become one with Christ.* The night before His crucifixion, Jesus sought to persuade His apprehensive and helpless disciples with a promise that reveals the Gospel. He said, *"On that day you will realize that I am in my Father, and you are in me, and I am in you"* (John 14:20).

Developing a healthy marriage starts with a promise to grow a well-built union with God through Jesus Christ.

The Promise

It is important to consider the framework in which the union was promised prior to determining the exact meaning of our union with Christ. The disciples were following Jesus for about three years. They believed him to be the King of the Jews, the Messiah of Israel. Like many of us, they believed that serving with Him would give them personal worth. They were earnestly waiting for the day when Jesus would establish His kingdom on earth, so they could receive the prizes (prestige, money, and power) by reigning with Him. The fact they had left their earthly means of security and importance no longer worried them so long as Jesus would actually raise up His kingdom now.

John 14:20 states the promise Jesus made to His disciples concerning their union with Him. Jesus' declaration, *"I am in my Father,"* refers to His being one with the Father. It is this claim by Jesus that separates true Christianity from all other religions of the world. Jesus did not claim to be just another good teacher or prophet of Israel; He claimed to be God! Being "in my Father," means what is true of the Father is also true of

Jesus because they are one in essence.

The thought of our unification with Christ does not come simply from this pledge of Jesus. The Bible reveals the same truth through *pictorial images.* As the vine and its branches are one, so are believers one with Christ. Paul uses three different comparisons in his letters to express the same promise. Believers are one with Christ as the structure and its foundation are one (Ephesians 2:20-22), as *a husband and wife* will become one flesh (Ephesians 5:31-32), and as *the head and the body* are one (Ephesians 1:22-23). The frequent use of the phrases *"in Christ," "in him,"* or *"in whom"* in the New Testament all reflect the basic promise that believers are in a vital union with Jesus Christ. It is from this union the believer draws incredible benefits of personal worth.

The frequent use of the phrases in the New Testament all reflect the basic promise that believers are in a vital union with Jesus Christ.

The Benefits

Utmost delight, achievement, and blessing are only possible when a couple is united with God and on the same spiritual path with each other. Since Jesus' promise is true, we can begin to appreciate the amazing special benefits of our union with Him by reminding ourselves that what is true of Jesus is true of us as well. *Was Jesus secure in God's love?* Undoubtedly He was, and *so are we. Was Jesus significant in God's plan?* Unquestionably He was, and *so are we.*

As we begin to identify and accept our union with Christ as true, we go into *the fullness of the Gospel of Jesus Christ in our daily lives.* Because we are one with Christ (we are in Him and He is in us), we are said to be loved unconditionally (Ephesians 2:1-10), totally accepted (Ephesians 1:3-6), forever forgiven (Colossians 2:9-15), important as ambassadors (2 Corinthians 5:17-21), meaningful in ministry (John 14:12), and adequate in power (Philippians 4:13). In short, our union with Christ meets all our personal needs to make us worthy *because He is worthy.*

Loved unconditionally (Ephesians 2:1-10)	Totally accepted Ephesians 1:3-6)
Forever forgiven (Colossians 2:9-15)	Important as ambassadors (2 Corinthians 5:17-21)
Meaningful in ministry (John 14:12)	Adequate in power (Philippians 4:13)

The Faith

Before we are old enough to imagine that there is a God at all, *we have been trained to trust in ourselves, others, and our situations to make us valuable.* As small children, we learn to *trust in our own performance* to make us noteworthy in this life. We also learn to *depend on the endorsement of noteworthy others* to tell us we are loved and, therefore, secure. These early learning experiences make it very difficult to later believe Jesus is the one who makes us secure and significant.

As adults, we fight the same kind of battle each day. When we sincerely ask ourselves what we depend on for our worth (i.e. security and/or significance), we find that we are trained from birth to trust everything and everyone but Jesus. In our innate form, what Jesus offers does not make sense to us either.

For instance, suppose I inherited a large sum of money. The money I received would generate a *false* sense of security as people begin to say they "love" me, they "accept" me, and they "forgive" me for any offense. Similarly, I might develop an *artificial sense* of value as I enjoyed a new logic of "significance," "purpose," and "supremacy" in my money. All my conditioning in this world's value system would tell me that I am now "worth" millions of dollars. Trusting Jesus, rather than the money for my worth, would be a great deal easier to *say* than to *do*.

The rationale that allows us to create and uphold a healthy sense of individual value is simply *faith in our union with Christ*. The reality is, as far as God is concerned, only those who are "in Christ" or "one with Christ" have any real worth as persons. *In Christ, we have everything needed to make us secure and significant.* Separated from Christ, we have nothing. The only thing remaining for us is faith. That is, we must chose to support our worth every day on our union with Christ. *"For it is by grace you have been saved, through faith—and this is not from yourselves, it is the gift of God - not by works, so that no one can boast"* (Ephesians 2:8-9).

Develop Your Personal Relationship with Jesus Christ - *Do You Know Your Pilot?*

1) **Our sin separates us from God and the relationship He desires with us.**
   God loves you and has an astonishing plan for your marriage. However, we all have the dilemma of sin in our lives. Every one of us sins and becomes separated from God. As such, we cannot identify and know God's love and plan for our marriage through our own efforts.

   "For all have sinned and fall short of the glory of God" (Romans 3:23).

   "It's your sins that have cut you off from God..." (Isaiah 59:2a, NLT)   .

   "For whoever shall keep the whole law, and yet stumbles at just one point, is guilty of breaking all of it" (James 2:10).

   "For the wages of sin is death, but the gift of God is eternal life in Christ Jesus our Lord" (Romans 6:23).

2) **Jesus Died for Your Sins.**
   "We all, like sheep, have gone astray, each of us has turned to his own way; and the LORD has laid on him the iniquity of us all" (Isaiah 53:6).

   "God made him (Jesus) who had no sin to be sin for us, so that in him we might become the righteousness of God" (2 Corinthians 5:21).

"But God demonstrates his own love for us in this: While we were still sinners, Christ died for us" (Romans 5:8).

3) Jesus is The Only Way to God.
"Jesus answered, 'I am the way and the truth and the life; no one comes to the Father except through me'" (John 14:6).

4) We must confess our sins to God and each other.
"Therefore confess your sins to each other and pray for each other so that you may be healed. The prayer of a righteous person is powerful and effective" (James 5:16).

"If we confess our sins, he is faithful and just and will forgive us our sins and purify us from all unrighteousness" (1 John 1:9).

"Yet to all who received him, to those who believed in his name, he gave the right to become children of God" (John 1:12).

"Here I am! I stand at the door and knock. If anyone hears my voice and opens the door, I will come in and eat with him, and he with me" (Revelation 3:20).

5) The Bible ensures everlasting life to all who individually accept Christ as Savior.
"God has given us eternal life and this life is in the Son. He who has the Son has life; and he who does not have the Son of God does not have life. I write these things to you who believe in the name of the Son of God so that you may know that you have eternal life" (1 John 5:11-13).

"I tell you, now is the time of God's favor, now is the day of salvation" (2 Corinthians 6:2b).

6) If you have a desire to receive Jesus as your personal Lord and Savior, pray this prayer:
"Jesus, I believe You are the Son of God and that You died on the Cross to rescue me from sin and death and to restore me to the Father. I choose now to turn from my sins. I give myself to You. I

receive your forgiveness and ask You to take Your rightful place in my life as my Savior and Lord. Come into my heart, fill me with Your love and help me to become a person who is truly loving— a person like You. Restore me, Jesus. Live in me. Love through me. Thank You, God. In Jesus' name I pray. Amen.

In-flight Navigation Checklist.

1) Do you thoroughly comprehend each other's spiritual beliefs and views?
2) Do you share your spiritual journey?
3) What is the origin for a person's connection with God?
4) How do you express differences in your spiritual beliefs for life and in your marriage?
5) Do you discuss difference in church preferences?
6) What spiritual beliefs do you want to pass on to your children?
7) Do differences in your spiritual beliefs cause tension in your relationship?
8) Do you think your spiritual beliefs will grow a stronger relationship as you face the challenges of life together?
9) Do your spiritual beliefs play a significant purpose in your promise to each other?

Introduce and Build Spiritual Confidence – *Fully Trust the Pilot, and You'll Arrive Safely!*

Creating spiritual confidence doesn't usually come naturally. Spiritual confidence can and most often:

1) Creates trust, oneness, and intimacy.
2) Diminishes disagreement.
3) Gives a sheltered spiritual groundwork for your home.
4) Fortifies your relationship through a common spiritual focal point.
5) Interjects expectation and enjoyment deeply into your marriage.
6) Encourages a home atmosphere of protection, tranquility, love, and forgiveness.
7) Introduces the basis to form a spiritual heritage in your family.
8) Permits you to experience what God has in mind for your marriage!

Where to Begin: Team up with God – *He's the Team Leader, so Fly with Assurance.*

Starting a personal relationship with Jesus Christ is the first and most important step in creating spiritual confidence. It's vital that both husband and wife are in harmony spiritually. That means both need to "get right" with God—they both need to submit to Him and follow Him.

The Lord wants you to summon Him into our life and marriage. He deeply longs to be the third cord mentioned in Ecclesiastes 4:12. God created each of us in His image with a soul to attach to the Spirit of the Living God.

As you begin your personal relationship with Christ, be prepared to share your spiritual journey with your spouse. Together, God will reveal all He has for you within the stunning pledge of a Christian marriage.

Praying Together as a Couple – *Praying Together Gives You a Strategic Planning Team approach.*

Praying as a couple is an essential component to a dedicated Christian marriage. The most intimate moment a couple can experience is praying with one another. Couples who pray together reconcile the question of who is the Lord above their marriage.

A study by David and Jan Stoop show only 1 in 1,500 couples that pray together regularly will get a divorce. However, only 4% of Christian couples truly pray together on a regular basis.[1]

When couples ignore praying together, they overlook an *enormous* opening to experience God's shelter, direction, and sanctification for their marriage! Praying together is both a solvent and glue.[2] It eliminates disgust and animosity while uniting hearts.

Swiss psychiatrist, Dr. Paul Tournier, says, *"It is only when a husband and wife pray together before God that they find the secret of true harmony: that the difference in their temperaments, their ideas, and their tastes enriches their home instead of endangering it...When each of the marriage partners seeks quietly before God to see his own faults, recognizes his sin, and asks the forgiveness of the other, marital problems are no more...They learn to become absolutely honest with each other...This is the price to be paid if partners very different from each other are to combine their gifts instead of setting them against each other."[3]*

At first, praying together may seem uncomfortable because we want our prayers to be personal. Praying with your spouse can make you feel exposed and insufficient. Prayer with your partner, although difficult in the beginning, will prove to be the best spiritual intimacy practice in your marriage.

Every Christian marriage needs a time and place where the couple can come together for a few quiet moments and focus on God. Couples, who are passionate about this part of their spiritual journey together, usually set aside a specific time of day and place to read the Bible and pray.

Obstructions to Spiritual Confidence – *Engage Your Tactical Air Navigation Aid.*

Satan is always hard at work in the hunt to avert triumph over your earnest needs for spiritual intimacy. As such, he leads us into disguising our genuine needs from those we love most, and he opens our vulnerability to spiritual attack. Satan despises couples living visible and godly lives.

Nothing intensifies spiritual closeness like transparency and forgiveness. A forgiving heart is the single greatest help in resolving past disputes. Couples must honestly face their suspicions and breakdowns. They need to seek God's wisdom and discernment for the spiritual vigor to resolve any aching encounters in their past.

Couples who completely discern God's unconditional love for each another begin to experience the oneness that God intended for their marriage. They then begin to restore some of what was lost in the Garden of Eden and are able to convey love, transparency, and belief in the oneness of marriage.

Finding a Church to Worship and Serve Together – *Choosing Your Seat and Row for the Trip.*

Decide on a church that teaches the Gospel of salvation with the following core *beliefs and practices*:

1) God created the world.
2) God created man in His image.
3) God the Father, the Son, and the Holy Spirit make up the Holy Trinity.
4) The Bible is the unquestionable Word of God.
5) God's love is unconditional.
6) Jesus will return.

The church should be reasonably close to your home to enable your active involvement and service.

Biblical References

Romans 12:6 – *"We have different gifts, according to the grace given us. If a man's gift is prophesying, let him use it in proportion to his faith."*

1 Corinthians 14:12 – *"So it is with you. Since you are eager to have spiritual gifts, try to excel in gifts that build up the church."*

2 Corinthians 6:14 – *"Do not be yoked together with unbelievers. For what do righteousness and wickedness have in common? Or what fellowship can light have with darkness?"*

Recommended Resources

Kennedy, Nancy. *When He Doesn't Believe: Help and Encouragement for Women Who Feel Alone in Their Faith*. Colorado Springs, CO: WaterBrook, 2001.

Strobel, Lee, and Leslie Strobel. *Surviving a Spiritual Mismatch in Marriage*. Grand Rapids, MI: Zondervan, 2002.

Graham, Billy. *How to Be Born Again*. Dallas, Tex.: Word Pub., 1989.

Chapter 02

Communicating
The Control Tower Is Calling

Pre-flight Information

Do we have a single method to communicate? Does how you express yourself always give the same message? Communication is the single most essential element in a relationship, a marriage, a friendship, at work or at play. It is the common connection to each trait of our actions, relationships, and purpose. Communication depends on the styles, patterns and skills we learn and develop. We have multiple forms of communication – spoken, written, non-verbal and visual are considered the four primary types we use to communicate.

Common Communication Problems – *Radio Transmission is 'Garbled.'*

There are many diverse communication styles, and being able to correspond with all types of people is an important ability. Communication problems in relationships can be the ticket to catastrophe. If you're dating, it's important to identify one another's manner of communication. Learn to speak his/her language, make them feel at ease and truly listen to what is being said.

You can conquer communication troubles in your relationship. Do the phrases "mmmhmm," "yes dear," or "whatever you say, honey" sound recognizable? All too frequently in relationships, we utter these responses to what our partners tell us. Occasionally it is the result of being momentarily sidetracked, but this response can also indicate the partnership has succumbed to some of the widespread communication difficulties in relationships. If addressed honestly and swiftly, such hurdles can be conquered. Keep in mind these challenges can also signify more complicated issues in the relationship.

Communication without listening is one of the most common

communication issues in a marriage. We often do not recognize our own inattentiveness, but tuning out your partner occurs more often than you believe. Engage yourself in the present and work at being a more attentive listener. We call it *Active Listening* and *Assertive Communication.*

People are generally classified as visual, auditory, kinesthetic-type communicators. Visual people are those who learn and communicate in a visual sense. They'll often use their hands to draw a picture when speaking. Sometimes they have difficulty talking on the phone because they're unable to see the person they are speaking with. Auditory people are those that like to hear things. They communicate best using verbal styles. They are sometimes sensitive to background noise and want assurance they're being heard. Often they'll ask, "Did you hear me?" People with kinesthetic communication styles learn best through touch. They're the touchy-feely type person. They respond best to a soft touch on the shoulder or knee that accompanies the words.

The way someone communicates is important. A passive-aggressive person may beat around the bush and hint at things rather than saying them. A confrontational person is more aggressive and likes to solve or talk about things as soon as possible. People with passive message styles do not like conflict and are vague in their statements. They rarely make decisions for themselves and avoid making waves when it is necessary to assert an opinion.

The Active Listening Process – *Tower, Did I Hear You Correctly?*

Active listening skills enable you to demonstrate your understanding by restating your partner's message.

Excellent communication depends on carefully listening to the other person. Acknowledge the content AND the feelings of the speaker. The active listening process allows the sender to know whether or not the message they sent was clearly understood when the listener can restate what they heard.

Examples of Active Listening: - *Roger, Your Message is Loud and Clear.*

"I heard you say you are feeling 'overwhelmed.' Although you enjoy being mom, you also need more time to be with me. You want to plan a time to talk about this."

"If I understand what you said, you are troubled because you want to go home for the holidays next winter, but you think I would rather to go to the beach. Is that correct?"

The Assertive Communication Process – *Did You Copy My Last Transmission?*

Assertive Communication is the ability to convey your feelings and ask for what you want in the relationship.

Assertiveness is a priceless communication skill. Successful couples tend to be quite assertive. Rather than assuming that their partner understands completely, they share how they feel and ask unmistakably and honestly for what they want.

Assertive individuals take responsibility for their messages by using "I" statements. They avoid statements beginning with "you." In making constructive requests, they are positive and respectful in their communication. They use polite phrases such as "please" and "thank you."

Examples of Assertive Statements: - *The Landing Gear Is Down and Locked. Ready for Touch Down!*

"I'm feeling overwhelmed. While I love spending time with the kids, I also want to spend time with you.

I would like us to find some time to talk about this."

"I want to go home next winter, but I know you like to go to the beach. I'm feeling perplexed about what choice we should make."

SPEAKER'S JOB: - Send out clear transmissions

1. Speak for yourself ("I" statements, e.g. "I wish...").

2. Describe how you would feel if your wish came true.

LISTENER'S JOB: - Affirm the broadcast

1. Repeat/summarize what you heard.

2. Describe the wish AND how your partner would feel if the wish came true.

The Imago Dialogue[1]

A more formal tool used in *Active Listening* and *Assertive Communication* is **The Imago Dialogue**. Developed by Harville Hendrix, Ph.D. and Helen LaKelly Hunt, Ph.D., it is a three-step method for communication: *Mirroring, Validation, and Empathy.*

Mirroring

Using "I" language, one person (the Sender) makes a statement that relates his or her thoughts, feelings, or experiences to the other person (the Receiver) such as: *"I feel," "I love,"* or *"I need."* Avoid shaming, blaming, or criticizing your partner and talk about yourself instead.

In response, the Receiver echoes the Sender's message- by paraphrasing—using a lead-in sentence like, *"Let me see if I understood you. What I heard you say is..."*

If the receiver correctly restated what the Sender said, the Receiver asks, *"Is there more?"* After this question is asked, the Receiver should wait for a response to show sincerity and desire to hear more. Often the partner might say, *"Well no...err...let me see...maybe there is."* Given more time, they will often go deeper and share more. That sharing can be the most fascinating part of the conversation as deeper feelings are revealed.

The Receiver may want to encourage this by saying, *"Wow, that's interesting. Is there more?"* The more the Receiver can encourage their partner that they are truly fascinated in what is being said, the more the bond with the Sender—even if the subject area is challenging or unfamiliar.

When the Sender says, *"No, that's all,"* then the Receiver can re-summarize with, *"So, in summary, I heard you say…"* It is important for the Receiver to make sure he or she has a clear understanding of it all.

When the Receiver mirrors the partner well, the Sender will feel satisfied that the point of view has been received and validated.

Validation

Validation can be challenging, especially if one's partner has a very different perspective on things. To connect as a couple, it's important that you realize and acknowledge that what each has to say makes sense to each other. In this part of the dialogue, creating that connection is vital. Who is right or wrong is less important. With the Imago process, you may find a solution regardless of who is right or wrong on the issue because the underlying pain is uncovered and can now be addressed.

After the summarization of the message, you can provide validation by simply saying, *"That makes sense to me,"* or *"I understand how you feel."* You and your partner don't have to agree, but should show respect for the other person's reality. Encourage phrases like, *"That makes sense to me because…"*

Empathy

In the empathy step, you want to imagine what the other person may be feeling, such as anger, sadness, loneliness, fear, joy, and so on.

You might ask your partner, *"I imagine you might be feeling afraid and perhaps a little sad too. Is that what you are feeling?"* Then if he or she shares additional emotions, the empathizer should mirror what was said, perhaps something like: *"Ah, a little excited too."*

In-flight Exercise.

The following exercise is intended to assist the couple with fresh communication skills.

There are four major communication styles: passive, aggressive, passive-aggressive, and assertive. The assertive style is regularly the most flourishing of the four. Couples can avoid difficult and indecisive conversations if they used the assertive style more often.

The following exercise should be completed separately. Use the following assessment to define your communication style. Then discuss the results with each other.

Communications Style Assessment[2]
In the midst of conflict with my partner, I tend to:

Communication Style (Weights)	Always (9)	Often (6)	Sometimes (3)	Rarely (1)	Never (0)
Section 1					
Stay quiet usually and don't express what I really sense.					
Seek ways to keep away from the other person.					
Quickly offer an admission of guilt.					
Be hesitant to wrestle for my contrasting opinion.					
Speak softly and patiently wait for my turn to speak.					
Avoid eye contact, or twist away from the other individual.					

Communication Style (Weights)	Always (9)	Often (6)	Sometimes (3)	Rarely (1)	Never (0)
Believe the other person's desires or demands are much more significant than mine.					
View myself as the origin of the disagreement.					
Feel powerless, disrespected, or angry.					
Dread that I will be discarded.					
Attempt pleasing the other person despite how it may affect me individually.					
				TOTAL 1	
Section 2					
Emphasize my position, believing it is usually superior.					
Slight the other person or their contrasting viewpoint					
Feel spirited and view my opinion as triumphant when I win the dispute.					
"Stare down" or look down at the other person.					

Communication Style (Weights)	Always (9)	Often (6)	Sometimes (3)	Rarely (1)	Never (0)
Elevate my tone of voice in order to get my line of reasoning across.					
Regard my perception as the best solution.					
On occasion feel sorrow or responsibility over the strategy I used to succeed.					
Consider the other person's standpoint as ridiculous, stupid, or unsupported.					
Disregard the other person's wishes.					
Command the path the conversation takes.					
Guard my rights while seeking to triumph at any price.					
				TOTAL 2	
Section 3					
Fall sort of my assurances due to situations beyond my control.					

Communication Style (Weights)	Always (9)	Often (6)	Sometimes (3)	Rarely (1)	Never (0)
Find it challenging to admit responsibility for disappointing others.					
Feel entitled to get my own way, even if it conflicts with "commitments" I have made to others.					
Not feel fully to blame for the measures that I undertake.					
Dread I will be discarded if I was pushier.					
Be afraid of argument with others.					
Want my own way, without having to be accountable.					
Feel offended by what others demand from me.					
Concede to others hastily, just so I don't have to deal with the problem any longer.					

Communication Style (Weights)	Always (9)	Often (6)	Sometimes (3)	Rarely (1)	Never (0)
Indirectly defy their demands by postponing or giving an unclear or confusing answer.					
Blame others for the dilemma in order to rationalize my actions.					
				TOTAL 3	
Section 4					
Be able to express my wants and feelings with assurance, straightforwardly, and completely.					
Be receptive to the other person's point of view, recognizing that they may have ideas, or thoughts, I haven't yet taken into consideration.					
Feel at ease agreeing to disagree with their point of view.					
Remain calm.					

Communication Style (Weights)	Always (9)	Often (6)	Sometimes (3)	Rarely (1)	Never (0)
Acknowledge the other person's position can be genuinely held by them, even if I don't fully concur.					
Make eye contact and properly continue it.					
Accept we both have beneficial contribution to the discussion, so I offer and receive.					
Recognize accountability for what I speak and how I state it.					
Feel upbeat about how I act toward others.					
Don't feel I have to "triumph" the disagreement every time.					
Control how I act, but not manipulate my partner's behaviors or opinions.					
				TOTAL 4	

Source: Adapted from *The Solution for Marriages*.[3]

Total the scores in each section and note the highest score. This is likely to be your primary communication style. Discuss the descriptions below and validate the results.

Total 1 = Passive Style Score

This communication style is characterized by an inability to override the demands of others. The person fails to see the options available to them and instead gives control to others. They avoid giving opinions on both major and minor issues and typically wait for others to give their opinions first. This person may simply agree or change opinions just to suit the other person, but often end up feeling helpless.

Total 2 = Aggressive Style Score

This style is characterized by attempting to get the other person to submit to them through verbal manipulation. They downplay the other's opinion as stupid or wrong. They are critical of the other's point of view and attempt to change others' opinions through intimidation, sarcasm or heated arguments. This style may seemingly be effective in the short term but often results in resentment and the loss of affection and loyalty from others.

Total 3 = Passive Aggressive Style

This communication style combines elements of both Passive (fear) and Aggressive (anger) styles, *at the same time.** Feeling angry, this person wants to retaliate but fear holds them back from doing it directly. The result is "disguised aggression." They resort to ways of attacking that enable them to not get caught, thus avoiding an open and candid discussion.

* Not to be confused with the person who alternates between passive and aggressive communication styles. The main problem for those who flip between the two is usually being too passive initially but building up to an explosion of intense anger before reverting back to the passive again.

Total 4 = Assertive Style Score

Assertiveness is a very valuable communication skill. In successful, vitalized couples, both individuals tend to be assertive. Assertive people don't assume their partner can read their minds. They ask specifically and directly for what they want.

The Impact of Communication on Intimacy

The following table shows how diverse communication styles impact intimacy in a marriage.

Communication Styles and Levels of Intimacy				
Communication Style				
Person A	**Person B**	**Relationship**	**Who wins?**	**Level of Intimacy**
Passive	Passive	Devitalized	Both lose	Low
Passive	Aggressive	Dominating	I win, you lose	Low
Aggressive	Aggressive	Conflicted	Both lose	Low
Assertive	Passive	Frustrated	Both lose	Low
Assertive	Aggressive	Confrontational	Both lose	Low
Assertive	Assertive	Vitalized/ Growing	Both WIN	HIGH

SOURCE: Life Innovations[4]

Biblical References

Colossians 4:6a – *"Let your conversation be always full of grace..."*

Matthew 12:35-37 – *"The good man brings good things out of the good stored up in him, and the evil man brings evil things out of the evil stored up in him. But I tell you that men will have to give account on the Day of Judgment for every careless word they have spoken."*

Ephesians 4:29 – *"Do not let any unwholesome talk come out of your mouths, but only what is helpful for building others up according to their needs, that it may benefit those who listen."*

Proverbs 18:13 – *"He, who answers before listening— that is his folly and his shame."*

Proverbs 10:19 – *"When words are many, sin is not absent, but he who holds his tongue is wise."*

Proverbs 17:27 (NLT) – *"A truly wise person uses few words; a person with understanding is even-tempered."*

James 3:10 (NLT) – *"And so blessing and cursing come pouring out of the same mouth. Surely, my brothers and sisters, this is not right!"*

Recommended Resources

Burke, H. Dale. *Different by Design: God's Master Plan for Harmony between Men and Women in Marriage.* Chicago: Moody, 2000.

McNulty, James K., and Benjamin R. Karney. "Positive Expectations in the Early Years of Marriage: Should Couples Expect the Best or Brace for the Worst?" *Journal of Personality and Social Psychology* 86.5 (2004): 729-43.

Parrott, Les, and Leslie L. Parrott. *Saving Your Marriage before It Starts: Seven Questions to Ask Before--and After-- You Marry*, Grand Rapids. MI: Zondervan, 2006.

Stanley, Scott. *A Lasting Promise: a Christian Guide to Fighting for Your Marriage.* San Francisco: Jossey-Bass, 1998.

Townsend, John Sims. *Who's Pushing Your Buttons?: Handling the Difficult People in Your Life.* Nashville, TN: Integrity, 2004.

Wright, H. Norman. *Communication: Key to Your Marriage: a Practical Guide to Creating a Happy, Fulfilling Relationship.* Ventura, CA: Regal, 2000.

Chapter 03

Managing and Coping with Stress
Depart on a Smooth Journey

Pre-flight Information

Stressors are outside experiences that cause an emotional or bodily response. The influence of the event depends on whether you view the occasion as encouraging or destructive. When stress levels are high or constant, it is common for physical symptoms (headaches, backaches), emotional symptoms (anxiety, anger), and relational issues (conflict, disconnection) to surface.

There are two ways to manage stress:

- *Remove the stressor.* Some stressors represent things that are controllable (working too many hours). In some cases, it is possible to make choices that actually eliminate the stressor (such as changing jobs).

- *Change your response to stress.* When a stressor cannot be removed, it is essential to look at how you react or control response to the stressor. Learning and then using healthy-coping methods can aid your respond to stress in healthier ways.

Stress tests are a valuable beginning for a person looking to reduce stress. These tests provide a chance to impartially look at your situation and decide how stress is upsetting your life.

Stress influences people in unique patterns; there is no common solution for stress liberation. Reducing the cause of stress whenever doable and studying useful techniques for managing stress is valuable ingredients in eliminating stress.

Common Stressors[1] – *The Fear of Flying*

Based on results from the first 20,000 couples to complete the Prepare-

Enrich Customized Version of the online relationship assessment, the top 5 stressors for each relationship stage are listed below. Overall, married couples report higher stress levels than dating or engaged couples.

1) *Dating Couples*

- Your job
- Feeling emotionally upset
- Inadequate income
- Your partner
- Too much to do around the home

2) *Engaged Couples*
- Your job
- Financial concerns
- Cost of wedding
- Lack of exercise
- Lack of sleep

3) *Married Couples*
- Your spouse
- Your job
- Feeling emotionally upset
- Inadequate income
- Too much to do around the home

Notice the number one stressor for married couples. *"Your Spouse"* was the number one cited stressor for both men and women. It is quite common for couples having conflict in the relationship to think the problems would disappear if their partner would 'simply change.' Not only do they think this, they most usually state it. Many marriage counselors find this finger pointing exercise employed in the beginning sessions of marriage psychotherapy.

Engaged couples are typically enmeshed in the numerous details of preparation for their wedding and reception. They also face the anxiety of a very high price tag attached to their nuptials. Planning a wedding is often the first opportunity a couple has to test their capacity to share major decisions and function as husband and wife. Finances, family, communication, and conflict are just a few of the many topics a couple will experience during their married life. The exercises offer a great practice field for their relationship. We devote an entire chapter to wedding planning boundaries later in the book.

Navigational Aids for Managing Stress

Healthy Ways of Dealing with Controllable Stressors

1) **Build understanding and empathy.** Identify and discuss the source of stress. Be sure you each understand what your partner is feeling and experiencing.

2) **Prioritize stressors to tackle first.** Focus on those things that are most important to you and drop the rest.

3) **Consider the dating stage.** Engaged couples may be preoccupied by wedding details; other stressors can offer a good framework to build vision and tools how their relationship will function, even after their wedding.

4) **Use assertive communication skills.** Many of the best ways to cope with stress often involve other core relationship skills such as healthy communication, conflict resolution, flexibility, and closeness.

5) **Ask yourself, "Is the circumstance really *that* important?** Will it matter in tomorrow? In a few years? In eternity?"

6) **What are the positives in this situation?** Choose to focus on positive factors, not the negative.

In-flight Checklist

Use the list below to identify the important issues you may be experiencing.

1) Choose those that apply within the past 2 years. *If the event occurred more than once, mark the number of times beside the score. For example, if you celebrated Christmas each year, mark "2" beside it.*

2) For each item on your list, determine which can be changed or resolved and which ones are out of your control. Mark either 'Yes' or 'No' beside each choice.

3) Prioritize the ones you can control and want to work on.

4) Discuss ways you can better cope with the issues that can't be changed or are beyond your control.

Life Events and Stress[2]

	Stressful Life Events	Able to Change? (Yes/No)	Priority	How to deal with the stressor	How to cope with the unchangeable stressors
High Level Stressors	Death of spouse				
	Divorce				
	Marital separation				
	Death of close family member				
	Personal injury or illness				
	Getting married/Wedding				
	Loss of Job/Retirement				
	Marital problems				
	Change in work shift				
	Family member health problems				
	Other				
	Pregnancy				
	Sexual difficulties				
	Drug/Alcohol abuse				

	Stressful Life Events	Able to Change? (Yes/No)	Priority	How to deal with the stressor	How to cope with the unchangeable stressors
Medium Level Stressors	Addition of a new family member				
	Significant change in finances				
	Death of close friend				
	Career change				
	Loan for major purchase				
	Foreclosure of mortgage				
	Change in work responsibilities				
	Child leaving home				
	Conflict with in-laws				
	Childcare difficulties				
	Spouse elects to begin or stop work				
	Returning to school				
	Other				
Lower Level Stressors	Disruption in living conditions				
	Trouble with boss				
	Change in work hours				
	Moving				
	Moving to a new school				
	Change in church				
	Sleep difficulty				
	Vacation planning				
	Holidays				
	Minor violations of the law				

	Stressful Life Events	Able to Change? (Yes/No)	Priority	How to deal with the stressor	How to cope with the unchangeable stressors
	Other				

This table is taken from "The Social Readjustment Rating Scale", Thomas H. Holmes and Richard H. Rahe, <u>Journal of Psychosomatic Research</u>, Volume 11, Issue 2, August 1967, Pages 213-218, Copyright © 1967 Published by Elsevier Science Inc. All rights reserved. Permission to reproduce granted by the publisher.

Biblical References

Philippians 4:6-7 – *"Don't worry about anything; instead, pray about everything. Tell God what you need, and thank him for all he has done. Then you will experience God's peace, which exceeds anything we can understand. His peace will guard your hearts and minds as you live in Christ Jesus." (NLT)*

Matthew 6:28-30 – *"And why worry about your clothing? Look at the lilies of the field and how they grow. They don't work or make their clothing, yet Solomon in all his glory was not dressed as beautifully as they are. And if God cares so wonderfully for wildflowers that are here today and thrown into the fire tomorrow, he will certainly care for you. Why do you have so little faith?"(NLT)*

1 Peter 5:7 – *"Cast all your anxiety on him because he cares for you."*

Matthew 11:28-29 – *"Come to me, all you who are weary and burdened, and I will give you rest. Take my yoke upon you and learn from me, for I am gentle and humble in heart, and you will find rest for your souls."*

Romans 5:3-5 – *"...but we also rejoice in our sufferings, because we know that suffering produces perseverance; perseverance, character; and character, hope. And hope does not disappoint us, because God has poured out his love into our hearts by the Holy Spirit, whom he has given us."*

Recommended Resources

Schermerhorn, John R., Richard Osborn, and James G. Hunt. *Organizational Behavior*. 9th ed. New York: Wiley, 2005.

STRESS Obstacle or Opportunity?, A. Pihulyk. Source: Canadian Manager (Summer 2001): 26.2, p.24.

Chapter 04

Conflict Resolution
Navigating Turbulence

Pre-flight Information

Many people have learned that conflict brings about an opportunity to resolve situations in ways that honor God and add benefits to those involved. Some people think of conflict as a tool to 'prove' their value, yet others view conflict as an opportunity to build strength and team work. The absence of conflict does not define a marriage, but the way conflict is resolved provides great definition.

The style a couple takes to resolve conflict will affect the outcome. The more positive the approach they take, the better the likelihood of victory.

Ten steps to navigate a turbulent flight.

When you have an issue that isn't solved through communication alone, go through the steps below. For minor issues, you can move through the steps fairly quickly. However, for emotionally-charged, difficult issues, you should move through the steps slowly and deliberately.

1. Find an appropriate time and setting to discuss the issue.

2. Decide what issue is going to be discussed.

3. Define the problem clearly from both points of view. How did both of you contribute to the problem?

4. State what pros and cons you can agree on.

5. Brainstorm together for possible solutions.

6. Summarize, compromise, and agree upon a plan of action to try.

7. Pray to God for help to take the necessary steps and to make progress.

8. Identify a time to meet together again to evaluate your progress.

9. Share and agree how each of you will contribute toward the solution.

10. Reward each other as the solution progresses.

NOTE: *If you continue to have difficulty or cannot find a way to solve the issues on your own, seek counsel from an elder, minister, mentor, godly friend, or Christian counselor.*

Is turbulence always bad?

Does the lack of conflict automatically mean you have a better relationship than those that do? No! Conflict isn't automatically good or bad. Sometimes couples worry that having a conflict means that they have a bad marriage. While we all would prefer a lack of conflict in our marriages, occasional conflict actually provides you with an opportunity to work together, learn from each other, and to love each other. Interestingly, having no conflict in a relationship may actually be an indicator that a couple is avoiding issues that need to be discussed. Ideally, then, seek to have the least amount of conflict possible in your relationship, realizing that when it does occur, you can find ways to work it through for your betterment.

When storms occur, be careful how and when you transmit it to each other.

Research shows that, 96% of the time, you can predict the outcome of a conversation during the first three minutes of talking![1] This means that harsh words early in a conversation can doom the discussion into turning destructive. In order to avoid this problem, use the model provided in James 1:19-20 where it says, *"My dear brothers, take note of this: Everyone should be quick to listen, slow to speak and slow to become angry, for man's anger does not bring about the righteous life that God desires."*

1. ***Be Sure Your Radio Is On:*** When working through a conflict, remember that your spouse wants to be listened to

and understood just as much as you do. Some researchers believe that up to 80% of relationship conflicts can be dealt with by using good communication and listening skills. Listening to each other and trying to understand where the other person is coming from is a practical way to show love, honor and submission to each other.

2. ***Transmit Slowly:*** The words we speak hastily when frustrated or angry often hurt others deeply. In the end, we often regret what we have said and wish we could take the words back. Remember, when you hurt your spouse, you hurt yourself. Many people think they need to "vent" their anger in order to deal with it. However, venting often leads us to spew out words or to take actions that are neither godly nor healthy. Rather, first rate your level of anger/tension from 0 to 10 (see the scale below). As our tension level goes up, our ability to think clearly and solve problems effectively GOES DOWN. However, most couples try to work through their most difficult problems when they are in the Red Zone! No wonder these conversations fail. Satan has a much harder time of getting an advantage with us when we deal with anger appropriately!

If your level of tension is in the Excessive Conflict Zone (8-10), don't try to talk out any problems right now. Take steps to calm down, such as going for a walk, writing out your feelings, working in your garden, and taking deep breaths. If you are in the Acquiescent Zone (4-7), be aware that you can quickly move into the Excessive Conflict Zone, so pay attention. Ideally we would always talk to each other from the Peaceful/Passive Zone (1-3) with a prayer on our heart and our spouse's best interest in mind.

0 1 2 3	Tranquil/Passive Zone
4 5 6 7	Modest Encounter Zone
8 9 10	Elevated Conflict Zone

SOURCE: Adapted from Apostolic Christian Counseling and Family Services

3. *Use the Trim to Stabilize the Aircraft:* When disagreements occur, pray! Seek for God's help in dealing with your feelings, understanding your spouse, and sharing your feelings.

Anger is often referred to as a "secondary emotion" because it comes as an outcome of another dilemma. When you are angered by something, try to discover which of the following categories likely prompted the anger.

- Emotional wound (e.g., humiliation, feeling of rejection, disgrace).

- Irritation.

- Fright.

- Physical pain.

- Inequity or wrongdoing (i.e., irreproachable fury).

When you find any of the above upsetting your responses, seek to resolve the conflict in a Christ-glorifying approach. Cooling-off, seeking God's wisdom by praying and talking through the conflict will usually resolve it. However, if you still have trouble resolving the conflict on your own, seek help and discernment from an elder, minister, mentor, counselor, or godly friend.

Issues versus Events: What are we really talking about?[2]

There are essentially two layers to most conversations:

1. Event: the topic at hand

2. Issue: the "under-the-surface" feelings, meanings, and goals

Many arguments are never solved because the couples are actually quarrelling about dissimilar unseen topics. Healthy, helpful conversation happens when dialogue is on the identical issue. A loving action (though often tough) is to acknowledge why your spouse is responding to a topic in a manner you understand. For example, a couple may have a disagreement about whether the napkin is placed under the cutlery or on the plate. They may both be talking about the napkin (the "event"), but the unspoken topic may be related to something very different. The silent issue may actually be, "This is the how my mother taught me," or "You never listen to my thoughts and suggestions." Always try to correspond on the same topic or issue. Many conflicts are never solved because the spouses are actually arguing about different hidden issues.

Avoid the Thunder Storms!

1.   People who are "conflict avoidant" in marriage will do just about anything to avoid an argument. While this may be a good quality in many situations, those who avoid conflict may also avoid bringing up important spiritual, emotional, and relationship issues. Those who are "conflicted/argumentative" in marriage may tend to provoke arguments from time to time. While you will always know where these individuals stand on an issue, they may speak words harshly and put others down.

2.   Jesus provided us with a perfect example for dealing with conflict. Sometimes He was silent or said few words, while other times He spoke quite firmly and directly. Jesus always spoke to the heart of the matter and always focused on the other person's eternal good. He did not avoid conflict due to fear of man. However, He did not seek to be argumentative. Thus, no right answer exists for every situation.

3.   Remember, sometimes remaining silent or saying few words is best, while other times you will need to lovingly confront your spouse. Note that if you tend to be "conflict avoidant," you will need to practice speaking in a firm and direct manner. However, if you are

more "conflicted/argumentative," you will need to practice holding your tongue.

Be Sure You Are Talking to the Correct Airport

Every couple, no matter how good their marriage, will have occasional disagreements, misunderstandings, and conflicts. Thus, when you have occasional conflict, don't be alarmed. Rather, take the time necessary to work through the issues and move on. Research has identified several types of conflict that can be so venomous to marriages that they are called the *"Four Horsemen of the Apocalypse."*[3]

1. *Escalation or Criticism -- occurs when spouses* negatively act in response to each other, continually offering slurs, character assignations, and personality insults, causing the conversation to become more and more hostile.

2. *Invalidation or Contempt* -- words or gestures that show your spouse that you are appalled and repulsed with him/her. Examples may be disdain, cynicism, mockery, name-calling, sarcasms, rolling your eyes, and so on. This often occurs when one partner slyly or frankly puts down the thoughts, feelings, or character of the other.

Negative interpretations or Defensiveness -- occur when one partner believes the others' intentions are more negative than is really the case.

3. Instead of listening to your spouse's position and talking through it, defensiveness is a way of blaming your spouse and often involves pointing out flaws in his/her behavior, opinions, and so on.

4. *Withdrawal and avoidance* or Stonewalling -- occur when one or both of the spouses, demonstrate a reluctance to get in or continue with important conversations. Withdrawing refers to terminating a conversation, whereas avoidance is an attempt to keep the conversation from starting. Stonewalling includes giving your spouse the "silent treatment."

The chronic presence of the four types of conflict listed above predicts divorce by 82%! [4]

Special Note: Emotional abuse (also called verbal abuse) and physical abuse are never acceptable and should not be tolerated in your marriage. These types of cruelty are sins that hit at the very heart of the marriage and provide Satan with an opening to tear down the marriage. While physical brutality may cause visible injuries, emotional abuse defeats a person's soul. Examples of emotional abuse include a chronic pattern of using hurtful words, anger outbursts, silence, isolation, gestures, threats, and so on. to control and manipulate another person. If emotional and/or physical abuses occur in your relationship, seek help immediately.

When to Seek Help

If multiple attempts have been made to solve a disagreement or if spouses are worn out from the corporal and mental hurt of their disagreements, then it might be time to engage the assistance of a professional or pastor to mediate and lend a hand to bring resolution and reconciliation between partners. More reasons to seek outside help might include:

1) Feeling physically or emotionally insecure.

2) Feeling verbally attacked or psychologically let down.

3) Fighting constantly about the same problem.

4) Either spouse expressing your anger on the children.

5) Either spouse using the children for emotional sustain.

6) Recurrent threats of leaving or divorce.

7) Feeling you no longer want the marriage or thoughts of infidelity against your spouse.

Avoiding the accuser-disconnecter cycle.

Spouses often have different opinions as to what is the proper way to settle conflict. Many times the wife feels the need to discuss the situation right away, while the husband needs time to think about it and talk later. This arrangement often leads to the accuser-disconnecter cycle.

For example, a wife may want to talk about why her husband has been away so much during the recent months. She may say, "Why are you gone so much? You rarely have time to help me around the house." He then says he wants to discuss it later and leaves the room. This causes the wife to become more annoyed and aggravated. She then follows him into the other room and unleashes a battery of additional questions. He perceives her questions as criticism or an attack, gets frustrated, becomes angry, and then shouts, "I work hard all day and this is all the thanks I get?!" He leaves the room and goes to bed.

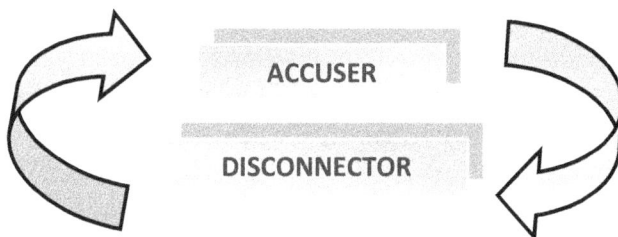

So who "causes" the accuser-disconnecter cycle? Is it the accuser or the disconnecter? In reality, both are responsible. When the accuser (the wife in this case) puts pressure on the disconnecter (the husband in this case) to talk when he/she is not ready, the disconnecter withdraws. However, because her husband didn't attempt to deal with her concern in any way, the wife became worried that the problem will never get solved and concludes that it is much more serious than she supposed.

The goal is to be more attentive to one another by doing the following:

1.   ***If you tend to be an accuser:*** Be careful not to be too antagonistic. Just because you think now is a good time to discuss an issue doesn't mean your spouse is ready. Instead of being persistent, let your spouse know that you have something you want to talk about and ask for a time and place agreeable to you both to discuss your concerns

2.   ***If you tend to be a disconnecter:*** Be careful not to leave without sharing a plan as to when you'll be ready to discuss the issue. Let him/her know that you are aware that he/she wants to talk, but now isn't a good time. *HOWEVER*, discuss a time in the near future (after supper, tomorrow night, over lunch, etc.) when both of you can talk out and address the issue.

Additional flight rules for good turbulence navigation.

1. Stay on one topic. Trying to resolve multiple issues in one setting can add confusion and more misunderstanding.

2. Don't dredge up the past. Bringing up past words, actions, and so on can be very hurtful to your spouse and damage trust.

3.   Avoid "You" statements. Starting sentences with accusations (even if they are true) will put your spouse on the defensive (like, "You never listen!").

4.   Use "I" statements. Speak from your perspective. "I feel frustrated when the garbage isn't taken out after I asked you to take care of it."

5.   *Control the tone of your voice. "A gentle answer turns away wrath, but a harsh word stirs up anger"* (Proverbs 15:1).

6.   Don't speak to each other or treat your spouse like a child. Remember, we are *"heirs together of the grace of life"* (1 Peter 3:7), and we should treat each other as such.

In-flight Checklist.

1.   When you were growing up, how was conflict handled in your family? How did your father and mother handle conflict?

2.   When you are upset, are you more likely to want to solve the problem right away or do you need time to think about it?

3. Do you think you are more likely to be an "***Accuser***" or a "***Disconnecter***"? In your marriage, what patterns do you think you should be guarding against?

4. How do you think Ephesians 4:26 applies to you as a couple? *"In your anger do not sin": Do not let the sun go down while you are still angry."*

5. Where do you fall on the continuum from "conflict avoidant" to "conflicted/argumentative"? What do you think this says about how we are likely to respond to conflict as a couple?

6. Are there any topics that you avoid bringing up because you are afraid they will cause a conflict or hurt your feelings? What needs to happen to make sure that these issues get worked through?

7. What types of things get your anger/tension level into the Excessive Conflict Zone? What do you do to calm down? How will you know what zone you are in?

8. If you start to notice any of the four types of destructive conflict in your relationship on a regular basis, how do you plan to respond?

9. If the two of you were having trouble solving a problem, at what point do you think you should seek out counsel from someone else (elder, counselor, etc.)? Who would you be most likely to go to for help?

10. Can you promise your spouse you will agree to go to marital counseling if needed?

11. As the spiritual leader of the home, what responsibility do you think husbands have in making sure marital conflicts and problems are dealt with? What is the wife's responsibility?

12. How will you know if something is bothering you and the two of you need to talk?

13. Are there any other ground rules for good conflict resolution you think should be added to the list?

Biblical References

1 Corinthians 7:28 – "*...those who marry will face many troubles in this life...*"

Ephesians 4:26 – "*In your anger do not sin*": *Do not let the sun go down while you are still angry...*" NOTE: The timing for resolving conflict is given as guidance; this is *not* a legalistic requirement!

Ephesians 4:29 – "*Do not let any unwholesome talk come out of your mouths, but only what is helpful for building others up according to their needs, that it may benefit those who listen..*"

Proverbs 12:18 – "*Reckless words pierce like a sword, but the tongue of the wise brings healing.*"

Proverbs 15:1 – "*A gentle answer turns away wrath, but a harsh word stirs up anger...*"

Chapter 05

Granting Forgiveness
Let God Navigate Your Heart

Pre-flight Information

We, as Christians, should be the most forgiving people on the planet since we are the most forgiven people in the world. Our experiences, however, tend to often make it complicated to forgive others authentically and wholly. We sometimes find ourselves using forms of pardon that is neither biblical nor remedial.

Can you imagine if God forgave you in precisely the manner you are forgiving others? Think of it this way: if the Lord responded, "I forgive you, but I can't be near you for a second time," just as you confess a sin to Him, how would you feel?

Many of us imagine that forgiveness is the same as letting the other person go "scot free." We will repeatedly endure the penalty of their indifference toward the event that caused us the pain.

As Believers, we must not ignore the connection between God's absolution and our forgiveness: *"Be kind and compassionate to one another, forgiving each other, just as in Christ God forgave you"* (Ephesians 4:32). *"Forgive as the Lord forgave you"* (Colossians 3:13b). God expects you and me to adhere to extremely high principles when given the chance to forgive others.

Don't Go It Alone! – *Never Fly Solo*

Our strength is never sufficient to grant forgiveness, especially if the hurt is deep and you were betrayed. We often pretend to mask the wounds with a smile, handshake, or other greeting, but the poisoning of the event remains deeply imbedded within. You must seek God's purification of your heart to begin building trust in the relationship.

Pray for His intervention to overcome the thoughts and feelings that continue to haunt you. Maybe your prayer will be similar to this:

> God, I cannot forgive him/her/them on my own. In fact, Lord, I don't want to forgive him/her/them; he/she/they don't deserve forgiveness. Jesus, my heart says to build a wall of protection so he/she/they cannot levy more pain and suffering. I know Your Word says to forgive seven-times-seven, and if not, the relationship between You and I will be fractured. Lord, I need Your strength and help so my heart will be softened and I no longer desire vengeance. Change me that I may forgive, as You forgave me, and love him/her/them as You love me.

God is anxious to answer your prayer. His grace to us will give new life and breath to allow us to grant grace and forgiveness to those who have harmed us.

Transmit Your S.O.S. *(Share Our Story)*

Has forgiveness been absent in your marriage or life? Maybe forgiveness is a big part of your life or marriage? Choose a difficult circumstance that challenged you in your marriage or family. Tell others how God brought you to forgiveness and restoration.

What Is Forgiveness? *The Touch-N-Go*

In order to understand what forgiveness is, we must first define what it is not.

Some people *incorrectly* believe that forgiveness:

1) Is a feeling
2) Is forgetting
3) Is excusing.

Forgiveness is none of those! Let's define each of these points to better understand forgiveness.

Forgiveness IS NOT a feeling. It is an act of our will. It involves making decisions. Our first decision is to acknowledge that we cannot forgive without God's help. He has to change our heart, cleanse our thoughts and give us Grace. Once we decide to accept His blessing, we (with our will) choose to no longer give license to the thoughts and talk about those things that have hurt us.

Forgiving IS NOT forgetting. Forgetting is a *passive process* that allows us to erase from memory, over time, the events that caused the pain. Forgiving is an *active process* (an action must take place). In Isaiah 43:25, God shares, "I, even I, am he who blots out your transgressions, for my own sake, and remembers your sins no more." He is saying He will no longer give attention to the sin, so we should do the same as we accept His grace.

Forgiveness IS NOT excusing. Excusing says, "It's okay." It says to the offender, "What you did was not wrong," or maybe, "You couldn't control it, so you couldn't help it." None of these could be farther from the truth. Since forgiveness is the pathway God is directing us, something wrong must have occurred. Because God has forgiven you and me, we must forgive the offender.

Forgiveness Is *(The Go Around).*

1) *A Decision.* **The decision to grant forgiveness may demand a great amount of effort, particularly if the offense is still fresh to us.** Make the first decision of forgiveness: Admit that you cannot forgive on your own and ask God to change your heart. Be empowered by the Holy Spirit and commit to forgiving those who offended you. Through forgiveness, God removes the barriers that our sins have constructed and He opens the door for a changed connection with Him.

2) *Unwarranted and Cannot be Earned.* Granting forgiveness may seem unjust because those offenses that need to be forgiven don't automatically "warrant" forgiveness. Albeit, we do not deserve God's mercy, but He constantly offers it FREELY. We cannot earn the love by deeds, actions, or words. The same

grace must be granted to the one who wounded us, no matter how deeply the wound goes.

3) ***The Opportunity to Glorify God.*** Explain that you are forgiving him or her because God has forgiven you unconditionally as well. Share the goodness of Jesus' death on the Cross and explain how His love is the representation for your forgiveness. This explanation may assure them, for the first time, what God means when He says, "I forgive you."

4) ***A Release to Him or Her from the Liability to Suffer Punishment or Penalty.*** Withholding forgiveness, focusing on the offense, being cold-hearted and unfriendly, destroying the relationship, imposing emotional trauma, spreading rumors or bad-talk, seeking revenge against the one who hurt you are all signs of un-forgiveness. Someone once said, "Un-forgiveness is the poison we drink, hoping others will die." You should tear down any walls that rest between you and a remorseful sinner.

5) ***Not an Automatic Release of the Wrongdoer from all the Consequences of Sin.*** Remember the rebellious Israelites and God's proclamation that they would die without entering the Promised Land (Num. 14:20-23)? Remember David's adultery and murder? This is not to say God will withhold mercy; it is to say He will quickly remove the separation of our sin and spare us the consequences of that sin. You may decide to remove some of the consequences of the wrongdoer's actions if they are truly repentant. (Maybe you lend an expensive jacket to a friend for a special occasion. Upon return of the jacket, you notice a large tear in the sleeve. The friend is unable to bear the cost to repair or replace it, but he is truly sorrowful. You elect to forgive and replace the jacket at your own expense, but decide not to lend anything to this friend in to future.)

How do I forgive? *Are You Ready for Take-off?*

In Luke 17:3, we find repentance should precede forgiveness. Before you rush off to confront someone, however, remember that it is appropriate to overlook minor offenses (Proverbs 19:11). As a general rule, an offense should be overlooked if you can answer "no" to all of the following questions:[1]

- Does the offense seriously dishonor God?
- Has it permanently damaged the relationship?
- Is it seriously hurting other people?
- Is it seriously hurting the offender?

If the offense is too severe to ignore and the wrongdoer has not yet repented, you may want to approach your forgiveness as a two-stage process.

- The first stage requires *having an attitude of forgiveness.*
- The second stage is about *granting forgiveness.*

Maintaining an outlook of forgiveness is unrestricted and is a pledge you make between you and God. By His grace, you search to retain a loving and merciful feeling toward the individual who has wronged you. This requires building and carrying out the initial pledge of forgiveness—in that you will not focus on the wounding episode or seek out retribution or reprisal in thinking, speech, or deed. Instead, you pray for the individual and are prepared at any second to receive complete reconciliation as soon as he or she repents. This stance will guard you from resentment and bitterness, even if the wrongdoer takes a long time to repent.

Five Compass Points for Safe Arrival (PAUSE)

"Giving in to others demands does not mean we forgo our loving concern. We must be aware of and lookout for our own interest and clearly know that responsibility. A person with wisdom rarely gives in to others without reason to do so. This wisdom will seek God-honoring solutions that are beneficial to many people. The process is known as Cooperative Negotiation or a combination of love and wisdom." [2] In Ken Sande's book, The Peacemaker: A Biblical Guide to Resolving Personal Conflict, he uses five principals for the acronym PAUSE:

1) ***Prepare*** – Preparation cannot be overlooked when reading for negotiation. Review ALL the elements available to you. Proverbs 14:8 and 14:22 may be good references to consider when reviewing. You may think it silly, but great attorneys win as a result of their preparation. You can accomplish similar success by praying, gathering the facts, classifying the issues, seeking Scripture principals, creating alternative solutions, expecting opposition, asking for a good time and place to meet, structuring your beginning remarks, and finally seeking Christian guidance.

2) ***Affirm Relationships*** – Conflict usually has two components: an individual and a dilemma. Many times we forget the emotions and concerns of others during the negotiation process. This most often adds to the anxiety and frustration, making resolution much more difficult. To avoid this hurdle, simply affirm the person during the process. The affirmation might be:

   "You are my best friend. We've known one another since elementary school, shared hardships, joy and disagreed. It's because I value your friendship that I want to bring resolution to this challenge."

3) ***Understand Interests*** – In order to understand interests, we must first examine the key principals: concerns, positions and interests. For example, a concern means to regard it as important or something interesting to do, while a position is a person's particular point of view or attitude toward something. Interests are the state of wanting to know or learn about something or someone.[3] These definitions demonstrate how often our thoughts and intents are mismatched.

4) ***Search for Creative Solutions*** – Better known as "brainstorming," this search involves everyone. Use imagination and creativity. Think of more than one solution, but it is important not to be afraid of combining ideas. Try not to conclude at this point. List at least 10 points that are possible remedies. For example, a couple cannot decide where they'll

live once they marry. Options might include: living at his apartment, moving into the home she owns, renting with friends, moving in with either parent, a travel trailer, selling her home and buying a condo, etc.

5) ***Evaluate Options Objectively and Reasonably*** – This is the final step in PAUSE. Now is the time to discuss and eliminate unworkable options. Listen carefully to each other, paying attention to objections and positions. Keep Matthew 7:12 in mind as the process continues. Let's explore the scenario in #4 above. The couple now begins to evaluate each option and removes the ones that don't seem to fit their dreams. After eliminating all but moving into either of the existing homes, they realize another alternative. They might rent out the home she owns to generate additional income, and then find a temporary residence until she finishes college and is more sure where her career will lead. They have narrowed the prospective solutions to three and now can decide the best fit. They've demonstrated their ability to recognize each others' differences, discuss possible solutions and develop an agreeable next step. Success!

If you have never used this approach to negotiation before, it will take time and practice (and sometimes advice from others) to become proficient at it. But it is well worth the effort, because learning the PAUSE principle will help you not only resolve your present dispute, but will also allow you to negotiate more effectively in all areas of your life.

If you're not able to come to an agreement, then set another time and place to continue. Revisit the steps above, keep searching, invent new options, don't quit. Should you come to a 'stalemate,' search for a mature Christian to observe and participate in the next session. Many times, the 3rd person can look past the agendas to provide wisdom and discernment beyond the negotiating parties.

Restitution - An Important Biblical Concept

When a person has hurt someone, the Bible states, *"And must confess the sin they have committed. They must make full restitution for the wrong they have done, add a fifth of the value to it and give it all to the person they have wronged"* (Numbers 5:7). Remember how Zacchaeus, the Tax Collector, was driven to repentance when Jesus came to Jericho? Zacchaeus wanted to see who Jesus was, but because he was short and could not see over the crowed, he climbed a tree. As Jesus approached, He looked up and ordered Zacchaeus to come down. Zacchaeus then said, *"Look, Lord! Here and now I give half of my possessions to the poor, and if I have cheated anybody out of anything, I will pay back four times the amount"* (Luke 19:8).

Restitution has several benefits. It restores the injured to the former position, society benefits by not profiting from unacceptable behavior, the offender has an opportunity to make amends for the sin, and exemplifies to society that he or she wishes restoration.

We see many examples of restitution throughout the Bible. Old Testament examples are found in Exodus 21:18-23 in regards to personal injuries. Deuteronomy 22:8 shares, "When you build a new house, make a parapet around your roof so that you may not bring the guilt of bloodshed on your house if someone falls from the roof." Exodus, Leviticus and Numbers provide great examples for restitution. The primary remedies for these sins are confession, repentance, and forgiveness in the Bible.

Many people argue that restitution is not a New Testament concept. However it is explicitly described in Matthew 5:17-20 and Jesus endorses it in Luke 19:10-10.

In-Flight Navigation Aids in Forgiveness

Think of something you recently did to offend your spouse and have not asked to be forgiven. Apply these concepts when asking for or yielding forgiveness.

In-flight Checklist

1) Is it easy or difficult for you to forgive a wrongdoing by your partner?

2) In order for you to be willing to forgive someone, what must they do?

3) Do you hold grudges toward your partner or others?

Biblical References

Luke 17:3-4 – *"If your brother sins, rebuke him, and if he repents, forgive him. If he sins against you seven times in a day, and seven times comes back to you and says, 'I repent,' forgive him."*

Luke 23:34a – *"Jesus said, "Father, forgive them, for they do not know what they are doing."*

Luke 6:28 – *"Bless those who curse you, pray for those who mistreat you."*

Colossians 3:13 – *"Bear with each other and forgive whatever grievances you may have against one another. Forgive as the Lord forgave you."*

Daniel 9:9 – *"The Lord our God is merciful and forgiving, even though we have rebelled against him."*

Matthew 18:21-22 - *"Then Peter came to Jesus and asked, 'Lord, how many times shall I forgive my brother when he sins against me? Up to seven times? Jesus answered, 'I tell you, not seven times, but seventy-seven times."*

Matthew 7:12 - *"So in everything, do to others what you would have them do to you, for this sums up the Law and the Prophets."*

2 Samuel 12:11-14, 2 Samuel 13:1-39 and 2 Samuel 16:21-22.

Proverbs 19:11 – **"***A person's wisdom yields patience; it is to one's glory to overlook an offense."*

Mark 11:25 – *"And when you stand praying, if you hold anything against anyone, forgive them, so that your Father in heaven may forgive you your sins."*

Recommended Resources

Kendall, Jackie. *Free Yourself to Love: the Liberating Power of Forgiveness*. New York: Faith Words, 2009

Sande, Ken. *The Peacemaker: A Biblical Guide to Resolving Personal Conflict*. 3rd ed. Grand Rapids, MI: Baker, 1997. Sixth Printing, October 2006.

Eggerichs, Emerson. *Love & Respect: The Love She Most Desires, the Respect He Desperately Needs*. Nashville, TN: Integrity, 2004. Print.

Smalley, Gary, and Ted Cunningham. *From Anger to Intimacy: How Forgiveness Can Transform Your Marriage*. Vereeniging: Christian Art, 2010. Print.

Rodgers, Beverly, and Tom Rodgers. *Becoming a Family That Heals*. Carol Stream, IL: Tyndale House, 2009. Print.

Kendall, R. T. *God Gives Second Chances*. Lake Mary, FL: Charisma House, 2008. Print.

Referrals

Love & Respect — This ministry offers materials, articles, and conferences designed to help those already married to enrich their relationship and, for those considering marriage, to prepare for the journey together.

Couple Checkup — An online marriage assessment to assist couples in discerning their strengths and growth areas.

Marriage Alive — The website of Dave and Claudia Arp, a husband and wife team who strive to help couples build better marriages and families.

Chapter 06

Managing God's Money

"Be on your guard against all kinds of greed; life does not consist in an abundance of possessions."

~ Luke 12:15 ~

Pre-flight Information

Money is essential in our lives! Did you know money is mentioned over 2,300 times in the Bible? Jesus talked more about money than Heaven and Hell combined. Most of our daily hours (nearly 80%) are consumed with working for, spending, and thoughts about money.

Sometimes we use our money to provide the needs of others, spend it in sharing God's Word at home and abroad, or use it to establish investments for our future. Money, managed improperly, can lead to addictive behaviors, be a caustic wedge in the marriage, and present an artificial sense of confidence.

"In this way I had more than two-thirds of my income available for other purposes, and my experience was that the less I spent on myself and the more I gave to others, the fuller of happiness and blessing did my soul become."[1]

~ Hudson Taylor ~

Both the management approach to finances and the lack of good skills to control their financial needs are considered two of the most frequently declared causes of marriage difficulties. Ron Blue and Jeremy White, authors of *Faith-based Family Finances,* quote a study by Citibank, the world's largest financial network: *"56% of divorces have finances as a major factor."*[2] Many times these discussions about money and finances create strife and stress for other areas of the marriage. Note: A 2010 study by the American Academy of Matrimonial Lawyers indicates that nearly 70% of all divorces have misuse of Social Media as a major factor.

Common Stressors About Finances – *Poor Maintenance Can Cause a Bumpy Flight*

1) Insufficient funds to cover debt over long periods can diminish sexual desire.

2) Financial stress can cause spouses to react angrily towards each other, using hurtful words and loud voices with the slightest provocation.

3) Money anxiety can lead to drinking alcohol more often, drug abuse, and smoking more.

4) Spouses may blame each other for the financial challenges, causing more arguments.

5) Persistent tension increases each person's threat of serious health problems, including depression, heart disease, and obesity.

Arguments over Money Can Involve:

1) Merging Funds

   o Philosophy among professionals vary from 'don't do it' to 'yes, it is necessary.'

   o Some couples struggle with the idea of having a joint account.

   o Some couples believe that banking individually helps them to maintain their financial independence.

2) Debt Management

   o Once you get married, you might take on your spouse's debts.

   o Unmanageable debt is often caused by the irresponsible use of credit cards.

   o Couples already married should try to quickly pay off any existing debts.

3) Budgeting

- o A budget helps you to track your income and expenses, and keeps you informed on what you can afford.
- o Men and women spend similar amounts, but each spends it differently.
    - ▪ Women will spend on groceries, clothes, and bills, but men might spend on the latest electronic equipment.
- o Having no budget results in unpredictable spending on things you probably cannot afford.

4) Investments

- o Work with a Financial Advisor to determine the correct investment strategy for you.

    - ▪ Discuss each partner's outlook on risks openly.
    - ▪ Review your investments no less than once per year.
    - ▪ Couple should discuss their investment goals together.

5) Financial Secrets[3]

- o Major amounts of credit card debt.

- o Financial secrets aren't a gender issue.

- o Giving money to the kids without the knowledge of their spouse.

In-flight Navigational Aids for Managing God's Money

Many couples think that obtaining more money will bring them happiness and achievement. Nothing can be further from the truth. Matthew 6:24 reveals the simple truth of money: *"No one can serve two masters. Either you will hate the one and love the other, or you will be devoted to the one and despise the other. You cannot serve both God and money."* Simply, you'll not be able to fully honor and serve God until you place your finances in the proper perspective in your life and marriage.

Every couple is subject to money related problems. Financial crises can sometimes occur, bringing financial hardship, enormous medical bills, major car repairs, and loss of employment. Many couples are not prepared and are then required to depend upon credit cards, loans, family and other means, resulting in huge debt. If this situation ever occurs to you, it is possible to dig yourself out, but it will take determination, uphill struggles and a promise to be better equipped for future financial hardships. You may have already overcome difficult times, now engage some approaches to better equip you for the next time.

Thirteen Biblical Principles for Sensible Financial Management:

1) **Luke 12:15** – *"Then he said to them, 'Watch out! Be on your guard against all kinds of greed; life does not consist in an abundance of possessions.'"* We are not to depend solely on money and finances. We must guard our hearts against greed and the desire to possess material items.

2) **Proverbs 28:22** – *"The stingy are eager to get rich and are unaware that poverty awaits them."* Seeking after money alone will bring hardship in the future. Develop the attitude of 'giving' and be blessed instead.

3) **Proverbs 3:9** – *"Honor the LORD with your wealth, with the first fruits of all your crops."*

4) **Malachi 3:10** – *"'Bring the whole tithe into the storehouse, that there may be food in my house. Test me in this,' says the LORD Almighty, 'and see if I will not throw open the floodgates of heaven and pour out so much blessing that there will not be room enough to store it.'"* Tithing is an honor and privilege. God gives us 90% of the funds we receive, asking us to return only 10% to Him. Many couples begin by using Malachi 3:10 and then increasing their giving every few months, awed by how God honors them for their faithfulness. If the tithing concept is new to you, challenge yourself. Give by starting out small. Increase that giving by a little and see what God does for you.

5) **Deuteronomy 8:18** – *"But remember the LORD your God, for it is he who gives you the ability to produce wealth, and so confirms his covenant, which he swore to your ancestors, as it is today."* God is the single source of our talents and skills to produce income. Man will fail us each and every time we begin to depend on the flesh. Our promise from God is still strong today—the same as it was for our ancestors.

6) **Matthew 6:34** – *"Therefore do not worry about tomorrow, for tomorrow will worry about itself. Each day has enough trouble of its own."* This is God's promise to us that He will care for us each and every day. We need not be concerned with tomorrow; tomorrow will bring challenges and trouble, but when we surrender it to Him, it will not be our worry.

7) **Proverbs 22:7** – *"The rich rule over the poor, and the borrower is slave to the lender."* Use borrowed funds with extreme caution. Borrow for only those items that will increase in value, not those that will depreciate.

8) **Luke 16:10** – *"Whoever can be trusted with very little can also be trusted with much, and whoever is dishonest with very little will also be dishonest with much."* Don't cheat the flesh or God. Dishonesty in the smallest way can lead to becoming untrustworthy with abundance. If we are faithful and trusted with the little things in our lives, God will reward us with blessing we have yet to imagine.

9) **Colossians 3:23-24** – *"Whatever you do, work at it with all your heart, as working for the Lord, not for human masters, since you know that you will receive an inheritance from the Lord as a reward. It is the Lord Christ you are serving."* If your work is with the attitude it is for Christ, not man, you will serve with a loving heart. Be joyous in all you do, knowing the Lord will be your source of reward, not that of the flesh.

10) **Philippians 4:12** – *"I know what it is to be in need, and I know what it is to have plenty. I have learned the secret of being content in any and every situation, whether well fed or hungry, whether*

living in plenty or in want." Learn to be content with whatever you have. This will be a huge step in your trust of God and of His provision. Remember, each day He provides our 'needs,' but not necessarily our 'wants.'

11) **Acts 20:35** – *"It is more blessed to give than to receive."* Be kind and work hard to serve 'the least of these' (Matthew 25:40). No matter how little or much we have, we can always make someone feel special. With a random act of kindness, not only will the recipient be blessed, but we too will experience a sense of reward.

12) **Romans 13:8** – *"Let no debt remain outstanding, except the continuing debt to love one another, for whoever loves others has fulfilled the law."* Always honor financial commitments. The only debt we should owe is that of unconditional love for each other, the same as Christ loves us.

13) **Proverbs 13:22** – *"A good person leaves an inheritance for their children's children, but a sinner's wealth is stored up for the righteous."*

"If I had not tithed the first dollar I made, I would not have tithed the first million dollars I made."[4]

~ John D. Rockefeller ~

In-flight Exercises

- Write down the material things God has blessed you with.

- Pray that you will seek God's help to change your heart to say, *"I have enough."*

- What is most precious in your life?

- Does your attitude toward money communicate your values?

- How much debt do you have? How do you plan to reduce it?

- Do you trust God to provide for all your needs? If not, which ones?

- How did your family values regarding money influence you while growing up? How are they affecting your use of money today?

When to Seek Outside Help – *When to Transfer the Controls*

Many couples delay seeking outside assistance on financial concerns until the frustration level reaches the critical point. Discussion of separation or divorce becomes the most dominant conversation after finances. Many churches have ministries to help. Others can offer Christian Counselors well versed in Financial Planning and Debt Management at no cost. (Caution must be exercised in utilizing the numerous organizations advertising Christian Debt Management, Financial Freedom, Debt Consolidation and more. Research their credentials, licensure and any complaints filed through your State Department of Business and Professional Regulation.) Regardless of your financial status, seek God's wisdom through prayer and reach out to a professional for solid advice, hopefully before the stress becomes overwhelming.

In-flight Checklist

1) Are the spending priorities considerably different than those of your spouse? What are the most significant factors that influence each of your decisions?

2) Have you both been completely transparent about your income, debt, expenses, and financial intentions?

3) Expenditures such as housing, insurances, vehicle maintenance, clothing, medical/dental visits, taxes, food, education and children will affect all marriages at some point. Have you discussed these at length and detail?

4) How do you plan to regularly discuss your debts and expenses?

5) Have you developed a budget and financial plan in detail? Do you need assistance?

6) Do you have any significant concerns about your finances today? What about the future?

Biblical References

Hebrews 13:5 - *"Keep your lives free from the love of money and be content with what you have, because God has said, "Never will I leave you; never will I forsake you."*

Luke 16:13 - *"No one can serve two masters. Either you will hate the one and love the other, or you will be devoted to the one and despise the other. You cannot serve both God and money."*

Proverbs 13:11 – *"Dishonest money dwindles away, but he who gathers money little by little makes it grow."*

Proverbs 22:7 – *"The rich rule over the poor, and the borrower is servant to the lender."*

Luke 21:1-4 – *"As he looked up, Jesus saw the rich putting their gifts into the temple treasury. He also saw a poor widow put in two very small copper coins. "Truly I tell you," he said, "this poor widow has put in more than all the others. All these people gave their gifts out of their wealth; but she out of her poverty put in all she had to live on."*

Recommended Resources

Blue, Ron, and Jeremy White. *Faith-based Family Finances.* Carol Stream, IL: Tyndale House, 2008.

Alcorn, Randy C. *The Treasure Principle.* Sisters, OR.: Multnomah, 2005.

Alcorn, Randy C. *Managing God's Money: A Biblical Guide.* Carol Stream, IL: Tyndale House, 2011.

Chapter 07

The Internet, Social Media, and Friends
Protecting Your Intercontinental Flight Path

Pre-flight Information

The introduction of The Electronic Age some 20 years ago has brought about many new challenges for marriages. Yes, I agree, the use of the Internet, Social Media, and electronic sources are now a 'necessity' in our daily activities. Managed correctly and properly, every couple can benefit from the sources available. A 2010 study by the American Academy of Matrimonial Lawyers indicates that nearly 70% of all divorces have misuse of Social Media as a major factor.[1] while a study by Citibank, the world's largest financial network suggests *"56% of divorces have finances as a major factor."* [2]

More people are connecting with a much broader circle of "friends," "connections," "loves," and other descriptors than ever before. We use social networks, text messages, and e-mail to stay connected, post events, advertise our businesses, and re-connect with folks from our past—some of these we even had previous love interests with.

Couples must establish and agree on boundaries to guard and protect the God-defined sanctity of their marriage. The temptation to connect with members of the opposite sex grows greater with each 'log-on' to the social network provider. The potential for being unfaithful is made extremely easy when the networks are used inappropriately. The bottom line: Your Social Media will become whatever you permit it to be. Guard yourself and your spouse. Sin and shame lurk at the next screen you view.

Here are some realistic guidelines to think about:

(1) *Visual Flight Rules.* Spending too much time on any activity can be harmful and distressing to your spouse. A significant challenge that married couples encounter today is finding quality time to spend with

each other. Unfortunately, many have no problem finding time to spend online. We have a friend who spends nearly nine hours per day engaged in some form of Social Media activity (Facebook, Twitter, Pinterest, and more). She now wonders why her husband has "shut-down" and is unresponsive to her.

(2) *Tactical Air Navigation Aid.* Social Media sites are not suitable venues to post grievances about your spouse or otherwise cause embarrassment. Always make it a point to demonstrate your marriage in a positive way – whether online or in any other public setting. Tragically, sites specifically designed to humiliate and embarrass people exist and gain popularity daily.

(3) *Traffic Situation Display*. Social media makes it fun and easy to share our lives with friends, family, and others. Because of this simplicity – not to mention the mysterious, flattering feeling that it produces – some people are often encouraged by sharing details about themselves and their daily activities. While this may appear guiltless and risk-free, it in fact has the potential to endanger the unique closeness you should be safeguarding for your marriage. Be thoughtful about what you share and with whom.

(4) *Runway Configuration.* Spouses need to be aligned regarding social network options. How? Simply talk about it! Is there current or potential online contacts or "friends" with whom either of you are uncomfortable? Do you have any communication styles that either of you consider 'off limits' to people of the opposite sex (e.g. email, private messages, chat)? What details of private and family information should be communicated online?

(5) *Coded Departure Routes.* Share each other's passwords to all devices and accounts, including granting each other unlimited, unannounced access. Will you have individual or shared email and social media accounts? Sharing passwords with your spouse indicates trust, openness, commitment, and accountability. It validates that your online connections are suitable—you have nothing to hide. Can you imagine any reason a married couple would not want to share passwords with one another? The answer to that question may be revealing.

(6) ***Out of Service.*** It is absolutely foolish to connect with former flames, romantic interests, or anyone with whom you have shared a past close relationship. Such behavior encourages a threat to your married life, not to mention suspicion, insecurity, or apprehension for your spouse. Unwanted advances from another person, perplexing ideas and feelings, and various enticements present significant risk, even if your motive for the connection does not originate from impure intentions. It is not worth the risk.

(7) ***Choose Your "Passengers" Wisely.*** Finally, it is your choice and accountability to agree on whom to add to your social media friends. Once a social network connection is complete, these people have fresh admittance into your life. Remember, you can always "unfriend" someone whose posts or interactions become bumpy or distasteful to you or your spouse. Any connection that can strain your relationship with your spouse is not a contact worth keeping.

"Maintaining privacy on social networks is much like hanging all your dirty laundry on a highway billboard—and then asking only your friends to look."[3]

~ Rich Mogal ~

Separate Your Flight Deck from Your Passengers. Customizing privacy settings varies by social media provider. Twitter has only one choice: On the Settings page, you choose your Tweet Privacy to guard your tweets (that means only the folks you 'approve' can view them). One of the most complicated providers is LinkedIn. They spread out privacy settings over nine (yes nine) different screens. Facebook purportedly simplified its privacy settings to 'just' four levels of menus.

Regardless of your social media provider, it is vital to discover how to navigate to the privacy settings. By the way, Google seems to be almost as friendly as Twitter.

Here's a partial list of the privacy settings to review and adjust to your satisfaction:

- Who can read your profile

- Who can see your posts and activities

- What information is shared with external sites and businesses

- Which applications can access your data

- What information your friends can share about you

- Who can see your pictures and/or location

- Which sites integrate with your social network (for example, Facebook's "Like" feature).

Most providers offer multiple levels of privacy: one for friends (or immediate contacts), friends of friends (or second-degree contacts), third-parties, and everyone else in the world. Each provider has a unique name for your connections (Facebook has "Friends," LinkedIn has "Connections," Pinterest has "Followers," etc.)

Most important is what you enter in your profile. Some providers make you think all the information must be submitted. However, there is no standardization that you must give the data. Here is a tip: If you don't want someone to see it, don't fill in the field. Review your privacy settings and your information often to ensure your privacy is set the way you desire and the information available to view is protected to your liking.

In-flight Navigation Aids on Social Media

Consider these potential areas to discuss:

1) Review your social media profile and pictures to make sure they properly reflect who you are as a married couple, rather than you individually.

2) Limit computer use to public versus private areas of the house.

3) Make it clear that you are married on your home page. Use pictures of both of you.

4) Don't get defensive if your spouse questions any of your activities. See it as an effort to protect your relationship. Help your spouse to realize, by your actions, that your marriage is paramount.

5) Commit to exhibit honesty, integrity, and full transparency in all areas of your use of social media, texting, email, and so on.

6) If you suppose something is not right, talk about your apprehension with your spouse, and if resolution can't be reached, seek competent leadership or counseling.

Biblical References

1 Corinthians 15:33 – *"Do not be misled: 'Bad company corrupts good character.'"*

Song of Songs 2:15 – *"Catch for us the foxes, the little foxes that ruin the vineyards, our vineyards that are in bloom."*

Job 1:8-9 – *"Then the LORD said to Satan, 'Have you considered my servant Job? There is no one on earth like him; he is blameless and upright, a man who fears God and shuns evil. Does Job fear God for nothing?' Satan replied. 'Have you not put a hedge around him and his household and everything he has?'"*

Ephesians 4:29 – *"Let no corrupt communication proceed out of your mouth, but that which is good to the use of edifying, that it may minister grace unto the hearers."*

Recommended Resources

Jenkins, Jerry B. *Hedges: Loving Your Marriage Enough to Protect It.* Wheaton, IL: Crossway, 2005.

Krafsky, K. Jason., and Kelli Krafsky. *Facebook and Your Marriage.* Maple Valley, WA: Turn the Tide Resource Group, 2010.

Chapter 08

How Cohabitation Impacts the Flight Plan

Pre-flight Information

Have you ever sneaked a look ahead of time at a gift you were going to receive (e.g. finding a birthday present and looking at it before your birthday)? Did knowing ahead of time spoil the surprise on the day you were to receive it? Living together is like opening a wonderful gift ahead of its intended time. It is unwrapping a special gift, peeking at it too soon, and then having to live with the consequences.

Cohabitation rates have skyrocketed since the 1960s when Western cultures began to cast off traditional sexual mores, but the same period also saw a correlating upsurge in divorce. This section looks at how a couple may have decided to cohabitate, issues that this has raised, and the impact cohabitation has had on their relationship.

The Bible says in Hebrews 13:4, *"Marriage should be honored by all, and the marriage bed be kept pure, for God will judge the adulterer and all the sexually immoral."* God has so much more in store for the couple who will stay pure in their earthly relationships. He also desires to forgive the couple who is willing to repent (turn away) of their sin and start their relationship anew.

The biblical commitment is always to sexual purity as God's will for our lives. Pastor Jeff VanGoethem says, *"The simple truth is that the practice of cohabitation does not follow God's wisdom on how to establish permanent love relationships. Little wonder they fail at the rate they do."*[1]

In the couples we have mentored, there is a dramatic difference in the spiritual and relational vitality observed between those who have had sex outside marriage and those who enter marriage as virgins.

Whether one looks at cohabitation from a biblical or secular perspective, the overwhelming evidence suggests that living together is not wise.

Cohabitation Facts – *"The Imperfect Flight Map"*

While virtually all studies show that cohabitation is detrimental to the marriage relationship, about two-thirds of married couples cohabit before marriage in the United States. Below are some relationship areas that researchers have found to be impacted by cohabitation.

Note that some recent studies[2] have yielded conflicting results for *engaged* couples that live together but have a specific wedding date scheduled. Even if there wasn't such a negative effect on couples, cohabitation is still morally wrong.

Higher Break up or Divorce Rates - *The Myth of "Test Flight Before You Buy"*

Today, a majority of young people believe that living together first is helpful in determining if a marriage is likely to last. Nothing could be further from the truth. While it might seem reasonable to "try the shoe on before deciding if you'll buy it," it's impossible to "practice" permanence. Marriages aren't shoes. Shoes can be thrown away without anyone getting hurt.

By its very nature, trying out a relationship through cohabitation results in a self-serving, performance-based relationship most likely to fail. That's a far cry from the commitment-based, covenant relationship of a true marriage. When cohabiting, couples usually focus on obtaining satisfaction *from* the other person. Marriage requires spouses to focus on providing satisfaction *for* the other person and receiving satisfaction as a by-product.

1) **Watch out for engine failure.** Cohabitation increases the divorce rate of those who eventually marry to about 65%.[3] Others estimate the increase in divorces after cohabitation at 50 to 100% higher than for couples who have not lived together.[4] This effect was noted in studies conducted in the United States, Canada, New Zealand, and several European countries.[5] Why is this so? Cohabiting couples fail to realize that what is *not* being tested is commitment—the very glue that holds a marriage together.

2) **The risks are even greater for African-American couples**. As reported in the *Journal of Marriage and the Family*, 70% of both white and black cohabiters believed they would eventually marry their partner. In reality, only 60% of whites and less than 20% of black cohabiters eventually married.[6]

3) **Crash landings are usually fatal.** Out of 100 cohabiting couples, 40 break up before getting married, and (with higher divorce rates) 45 of the 60 who do marry get divorced. This leaves only 15 of 100 couples still together ten years later. Cohabitation isn't a "trial marriage" but rather a "trial divorce."[7]

4) **A University of Western Ontario study** of over 8,000 never married men and women found a direct relationship between cohabitation and divorce. It was determined that cohabitation "has a direct negative impact on subsequent marital stability," because living in such a union "undermines the legitimacy of formal marriage" and "reduces commitment of marriage."[8]

5) **Dr. Scott Stanley from the University of Denver** reported in his book, *The Power of Commitment*, that "men were less dedicated in their marriages if they had lived with their partners before marriage."[9] If a couple lives together before marriage, both partners are more likely to cheat on the other after marriage.

6) **The longer the 'in-flight' (cohabitation) experience, the more likely married individuals are to question the value of marital permanence.** Couples who do not cohabit prior to marriage, on the other hand, are more likely to accept that various small stressors are part of the normal cost of commitment to marital permanence.[10]

Adverse Psychological Impact – *"Intellectual Turbulence"*

1) Cohabiting women have rates of depression three times higher than married women (National Institute for Mental Health).[11] The longer couples cohabit, the greater the likelihood of depression.[12]

2) A study by the National Council on Family Relations (based on 309 newlywed couples) found those who cohabited were less happy in marriage.[13]

3) Our discussions with cohabiting couples indicate that women tend to view living together as a stepping stone to marriage while the appeal to their male partners was the convenience of readily available sex and shared expenses. This difference in perspective often leads to grave disappointment to cohabiting women.

Reduced Communication - *"It's Hard to Hear the Control Tower"*

1) Dr. Catherine Cohan and Stacey Kleinbaum of Pennsylvania State University interviewed 92 couples married less than 2 years and found that those who lived together for *just one month* before marriage displayed poorer communication and problem-solving skills than those who did not live together. "In general, they discovered that those who lived together before marriage were more verbally aggressive, more hostile, and less supportive than those who waited until marriage to live together. The problem, according to the authors, could be that those living together without the benefit of marriage have less commitment to one another and so they don't work at their marriage as much. They summed up their research by saying, 'We just know that people who lived together first had poorer communication skills."[14]

2) 60% of those who had cohabited before marriage were more verbally aggressive, less supportive of one another, and more hostile than the 40% of spouses who had not lived together.[15]

3) People who lived together before marriage have more negative communication in their marriages than those who did not live together.[16]

Reduced Relationship Quality – *"Stormy Weather Is Ahead"*

1) Cohabitation is associated with lower levels of relationship satisfaction.[17]

2) Cohabitation is associated with higher perceived relationship instability.[18]

3) Cohabitation is associated with lower levels of dedication to the partner for both men and women.[19]

4) Conventional wisdom says it is acceptable to have a "trial period" to "test drive a car before you buy it." For marriage, however, just the opposite is true! "A newly married couple makes a more deliberate effort to accommodate each other because they know their relationship will be for life. They want to build compatibility, not test it."[20] As Proverbs 14:12 reminds us, "There is a way that seems right to a man, but in the end it leads to death."

5) The longer couples live together before marriage, the earlier disillusionment develops in the marital relationship along with lower the marital quality and commitment. [21]

Increased Aggression – *"Lightning and Thunder Can Abort the Mission"*

1) Cohabitation is associated with greater likelihood of domestic aggression.[22]

2) A woman who lives with a man is 3 times more likely to be physically abused than a married woman, and if the cohabitating couple breaks up, the woman is 18 times more likely to be harmed than a married woman.[23]

3) Physical intimacy is a mistaken attempt to quickly build emotional bridges, but relationships built on such an inadequate foundation eventually collapse. A study at Penn State University comparing the relationship qualities of 682 cohabiters and 6,881

married couples, 19 to 48 years of age, found that cohabiters argue, shout, and hit more often than married couples.[24]

4) A random sampling of marriages found that 60% had cohabitated before marriage. The studies found that these 60% were more likely to be verbally aggressive, less supportive of one another, and more hostile than the 40% who had not lived together.[25]

Handling of Property - *Baggage Claims*

Economic forces often contribute to a couple deciding to cohabit.

1) "A couple dates, they get sexually involved, and they find themselves spending a great deal of time together, including many nights. Sooner or later it dawns on them that they can do what they're doing much cheaper by sharing a residence and other living expenses. Their thinking has severed the moral connection between sex and marriage so the economic aspect of their relationship becomes the dominant consideration."[26]

2) For most cohabiting couples, money and property tend to remain either 'his' or 'hers,' rather than 'ours'. As a result, there is limited shared financial goal setting and planning with less importance placed on how he or she spends their own money. This mindset misses the economic synergy that is present in most marriages.

Adverse Impact on Children – *"The Flight Crew Is in Danger"*

1) "Compared with children in married stepfamilies, children in cohabiting homes are more likely to fail in school, run afoul of the law, suffer from depression, do drugs, and—most disturbingly—be abused. (Note that children in in-tact, married homes do best on all these outcomes.) In the words of an Urban Institute study, "cohabiting families are not simply an extension of traditional married biological or blended families. Indeed, a recent federal report on child abuse found that children in cohabiting stepfamilies were 98% more likely to be physically abused, 130% more likely to be sexually abused, and 64% more

likely to be emotionally abused, compared with children in married stepfamilies."[27]

2) Research reported on a website for husbands and fathers showed:[28]

- Since cohabiting couples are more likely to break up than married couples, children are five times more likely to experience the trauma of a breakup of their parents (Journal of Marriage and Family).

- Children are 50 times more likely to be abused when they are not living with two biological or adoptive parents (U.S. Census data).

- Even factoring in socioeconomic and mental health differences, the children of cohabiting couples are twice as likely to suffer from psychiatric disorders, diseases, suicide attempts, alcoholism, and drug abuse.

- Children are more likely to suffer the negative effects of poverty and low socioeconomic status.

- Children are more likely to have difficulties forming healthy relationships.

3) Parents who cohabited have greater difficulty establishing moral guidelines for their children, especially when they reach the dating age.

Cohabitation without Sex – *"Flying without Fuel"*

While most couples living together before marriage are sexually involved, what about a cohabiting couple that is not sexually active? For example, how do you mentor a couple that lives together for financial reasons but chooses to abstain from sex until marriage?

While we applaud a couple's decision to abstain sexually before marriage, there are still several good reasons why a couple shouldn't live together before marriage.

1) *The first issue is* **temptation**. Let's face it; living together, sharing a house, or sharing a bed is not the best way to fight temptation. If you are serious about saving all sexual activity for marriage, the last thing you should do is move in with the person you love and are sexually attracted to. When you live together before marriage, you increase your exposure and vulnerability to temptation. *"Can a man scoop fire into his lap without his clothes being burned?"* (Proverbs 6:27). In a cohabiting arrangement, ask yourself, are you truly relating to each other like brother and sister with absolute purity? *"Treat younger men as brothers... and younger women as sisters, with absolute purity"* (1 Timothy 5:1-2).

2) *Next is the matter of your* **testimony**. The Bible says to avoid even the *appearance* of evil (Ephesians 5:3; 1 Thessalonians 5:22). What kind of example does cohabitation set for others who are watching? How will those who do not know about your commitment to abstain sexually view your relationship to each other and to Christ? The testimony of our lives affects how people view Christ, the church, and God's design for marriage. Many have rejected Christianity because they don't see people who call themselves Christian living it out. Living together presents a poor testimony for Christ and His church. *"I urge you to live a life worthy of the calling you have received"* (Ephesians 4:1b).

   You also present a stumbling block to others who may be encouraged to follow in your footsteps without abstaining from sex. *"Make up your mind not to put any stumbling block or obstacle in your brother's way"* (Romans 14:13b).

3) *Thirdly there is the trivialization* **of marriage.** Living together trivializes marriage by detracting from the sacredness that God ordained for marriage alone. Living together prematurely adopts the social and some of the relational aspects of marriage and therefore dishonors it. This goes against Hebrews 13:4 which says, *"Let marriage be honored by all."* It's sad to hear a couple who cohabited and then gets married say, "It's not that

different." They have lost out on an important part of the joy and uniqueness of the marriage relationship which God intended for them.

Additionally, the trivialization effect has been found to adversely impact the couple's relational dynamics in several areas.

4) *When you get married, you are likely to have more difficulty with the transition.* While abstaining sexually before marriage is always a wise choice, the limited difference in living arrangements between the day before and the day after the wedding can make it more difficult to suddenly "let go" sexually after abstaining during cohabitation.

If you ever decide to break your engagement, your heartache, financial, and even legal complications will be that much greater since you have emotionally and physically bonded to a greater extent than you would have if you didn't cohabit.

In-flight Checklist.

1) How are you dealing with the challenges of living together?

2) How familiar are you with the research on the impact of cohabitation on a couple's long-term prospects for lasting relationship?

3) How has living together impacted your level of lifelong commitment to each other?

4) Has your level of confidence in the strength of your relationship changed since you began cohabiting?

5) Was the step you took to live together something you specifically planned or did you just drift into that decision?

6) How did you reconcile your religious teaching and spiritual beliefs with your decision to cohabitate?

7) How have your families reacted to your decision to live together?

Recommended Resources

McManus, Michael J., and Harriett McManus. *Living Together: Myths, Risks & Answers*. New York: Howard, 2008.

Whitehead, PhD, Barbara Dafoe, and David Popenoe. "Publications - Special Reports, The National Marriage Project, U.Va." *University of Virginia*. University of Virginia, 28 Apr. 2004. http://www.virginia.edu/marriageproject/pdfs/print_whitehead_testimoni al.pdf.

Institute for American Values, and National Center for African American Marriages and Parenting. *The Marriage Index A Proposal to Establish Leading Marriage Indicators*. 1st ed. Poulsbo, WA: Broadway Pubns, 2009.

Chapter 09

The Wedding Day Plans
Planning Your Take-off

Pre-flight Information

Planning a wedding is probably the most stressful event you will experience in the early stage of your 'married life.' Conflicts are a given! Managing those discussions sometimes involve not just the couple, but their families as well. Parents, friends, and family attempt to offer suggestions they think can be helpful, but often those ideas become unrealistic, costly and not-at-all what the couple's expectation is for their special day. Couples should dedicate considerable time discussing their desires for life together and how they expect to incorporate these expectations into the wedding day event.

Well-known Problems during Wedding Planning – *Severe Weather Avoidance Plan (SWAP)*

SWAP is normally implemented to provide the least disruption to the Air Traffic Control system when flight through portions of airspace is difficult or impossible due to severe weather. Consider how you can implement your SWAP during the storms of these challenges:

1) Wedding budgets.

2) Your expectations are different than your family and friends.

3) Differences in family and cultural beliefs.

4) Who to invite, how many?

5) Where to have the ceremony.

What to Do Next - *Implementing the Ground Stops*

When your wedding planning process becomes an overwhelming, seemingly insurmountable stressor, you may want to consider a temporary Ground Stop. Simply pause and change course until you are refreshed and able to implement a better solution or route.

1) Make your plans based on your expectations as a couple.

2) The wedding day "is your day." However, be considerate of those closest to you.

3) How will each of you take ownership in the planning?

   - Make decisions together

   - Decide who is best to explore and negotiate areas such as:

     - Rehearsal dinner location

     - Reception venue and menu

     - Honeymoon travel and location

4) Circle back and decide together on ALL elements after each of you have explored the possibilities.

5) Consider engaging a Wedding Planner to assist with details

Wedding Etiquette – *Flight Schedule Monitor*

Shocking, but true, Wedding Etiquette is pretty much gone. Question most wedding vendors and they'll confirm that today's weddings are pretty much "anything goes." Explore the thousands of websites providing advice from invitations, to themes, to colors, to checklists. Discussions are endless and sometimes contradictory between authors and forums. Thus you, the couple, must discern what is best for you. Simply expecting a single standard does not exist.

Some items you may want to examine and then define your expectation:

1) Hotel rooms for guests – who pays?
2) Bridesmaids/Groomsmen expenses – how much, payment by whom?

3) Indoor or outdoor ceremony
4) Thank you notes – who receives and who does not.
5) Gifts for parents
6) The Bride and Groom gift exchange

Questions Before Take-off

1) How do you plan to reflect God to others on your wedding day?

2) Twenty-five years from now, what will be the single most important memory of your wedding day?

3) Have you sought God's heart in each planned decision? Why or why not?

In-Flight Checklist

1) How is the current planning process working for you?

2) Is each of you participating in the planning?

3) How can you better utilize the attributes of your fiancé in the planning process?

Recommended Resources

Doherty, William J., and Elizabeth Doherty. *Take Back Your Wedding: Managing the People Stress of Wedding Planning.* [S.l.]: urge, 2007.

Olson, David H. L., Amy Olson-Sigg, and Peter J. Larson. *The Couple Checkup.* Nashville, TN: Thomas Nelson, 2008.

Eggerichs, Emerson. *Love & Respect: The Love She Most Desires, the Respect He Desperately Needs.* Nashville, TN: Integrity, 2004.

Biblical References

Ephesians 5:31-32 – *"For this reason a man will leave his father and mother and be united to his wife and the two will become one flesh. This is a profound mystery--but I am talking about Christ and the church."*

Philippians 2:3-4 – *"Do nothing out of selfish ambition or vain conceit, but in humility consider others better than yourselves. Each of you should look not only to your own interests, but also to the interests of others."*

Ephesians 5:25 – *"Husbands, love your wives, just as Christ loved the church and gave himself up for her."*

Chapter 10

The Holidays
Book Your Travel Plans Early

Pre-flight Information

Couples can come upon a lot of stress on what, how, when and where to celebrate the holidays. Common stressors are the differing expectations of parents and in-laws, brothers and sisters, extended or blended families, employers, and even friends. Blend these ingredients with those who don't recognize or respect the desires of a newly married couple and you have a recipe for catastrophe.

What Causes Holiday Stress? – *Unsafe Flight Paths*

1) Finances.

2) Memories of Lost Loved Ones.

3) Too Many Activities.

4) Eating Too Much.

5) Aloneness.

6) Family Togetherness.

Minimizing the Holiday Stress – *Check the forecast before you begin the trip.*

Holiday stress is totally predictable. Holiday stress will begin and end. Unlike other types of negative stress we encounter in life, we can make plans to minimize the holiday stress and the negative impact upon us.

Below are some tips you can use to help reduce holiday stress before it begins.

1) **Set Your Priorities.** It's important to decide what traditions share the most positive impact and eliminate unnecessary activities. For example, if you typically become weighed down by baking, caroling, shopping, sending cards, and visiting relatives, you may want to pick a few favorite activities and really enjoy them and omit the rest.

2) **Change Your Expectations for Togetherness.** It's vital to be aware of your limitations. Reflect on former years and attempt to try and identify how much togetherness you and your family can tolerate before feeling negative stress. It is okay to set limits on what you are and are not willing to do, including forgoing your visits or limiting them to every other year.

3) **Set a Schedule.** Putting your plans on paper can show you how realistic they are. If you find a day planner, fill in the hours with scheduled activities; you will be able to see if you're trying to bundle in too much. Start with your highest priorities; be sure to schedule in some time to take a "me-time break" each day such as exercise or just a "time-out." Plan ahead. Set aside specific days for shopping, holiday wrapping, cooking, and so on.

4) **Acknowledge Your Feelings.** If you have recently experienced a tragedy or you can't be with those you cherish, realize that it's absolutely normal to feel sorrow and heartache. It's okay to take time to shed tears and convey your thoughts. It's unrealistic to force happiness just because it's the holiday season.

5) **Be Realistic.** Don't expect perfection in the holiday spirit. Families change and grow; traditions and customs often adjust as well. Select the most treasured to cling to and expect new ones to develop. For example, if your child is away at college and unable to come home, exchange videos and photos or engage in face-to-face type electronic communication methods. The spirit of the holiday can be joyous if you accept the changes.

6) **Set Aside Differences.** Family members and friends who don't meet your expectations should be extended courtesy and respect

during the holidays. Try to accept them for who they are, and they'll return the kindness to you as well. Be thoughtful when relatives or friends are disturbed when something doesn't go as planned. Not only are you feeling uncomfortable, but most likely they are feeling the holiday stress also.

7) **Stick to a Budget.** Decide how much you can afford to spend and then stick to your budget. Happiness doesn't come with a mountain of expensive gifts. Maybe something 'homemade' will give pleasure to both you and the recipient. Alternatives could be to give a contribution to a charity in honor of a loved one, initiate a family gift exchange with spending limits, encourage your friends and family to adopt-a-family, and create a neighborhood Angel Tree for the community children.

8) **Learn to Say Yes or No. Matthew 5:37** says, *"All you need to say is simply 'Yes' or 'No'; anything beyond this comes from the evil one."* Saying yes when you should say no can make you feel angry and besieged. Friends and colleagues should understand if you're not able to take part in every plan or festivity.

9) **Don't Abandon Healthy Habits.** Overindulgence adds to your stress and guilt. Holiday celebrations bring many opportunities to indulge in excess, such as alcohol, food, spending, and much more. Eat a healthy snack before holiday parties so that you don't go overboard on sweets, cheese or drinks. Continue to get plenty of sleep and physical activity.

10) **Take a Breather.** Make some time for yourself. Spending just 15 minutes of "I time" without distractions may reenergize you sufficiently to properly navigate all you need to do. Take a walk, jog a mile, get quiet with God, or listen to soothing music. These activities, or others you like best, will release stress by clearing your mind, slowing your breathing and restoring inner calm.

11) **Seek Professional Help If You Need It.** Despite your best efforts, you may find yourself feeling tirelessly sad or worried, inundated by physical ailments, suffering from sleeplessness,

experiencing irritability and hopeless, and unable to face routine chores. If these feelings last for a while, talk to your doctor or a mental health professional.

Take Control of the Holidays – *Get Control of the Plane*

Don't let your celebrations become something you fear. As an alternative, take preventative measures to manage the stress and depression that can ruin the holidays. Know your holiday triggers so you can rectify them before they become problematic. With a little preparation and some optimistic ideas, you can find happiness and enjoyment during the holidays.

A study by Mental Health America (formerly known as the National Mental Health Association) revealed the top six holiday stressors— finances and loss of loved ones topping the list.

"The holiday season can be a challenging time of year," said David Shern, Ph.D., president and CEO of Mental Health America. *"Being aware of stressors and taking steps towards managing them is essential to making the holiday season healthy. Neglecting them, on the other hand, can abate a person's well-being and overall health."*

"Americans are stressed during the holidays - we've long known this," said Shern. *"However, on January 2, when a person may expect the stress let up, they instead find themselves feeling down, physically ill or anxious. This is because stress takes a serious toll on a person's overall health - both 'physical' and 'mental'. We need to help people manage stress better - they'll feel better, they'll be healthier and they'll probably enjoy the holidays better."*

SOURCES OF HOLIDAY STRESS[1]

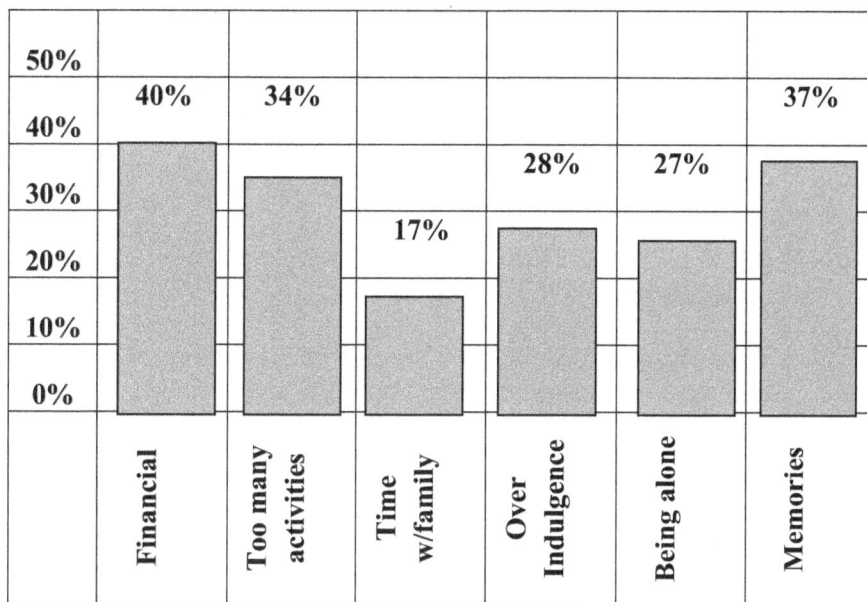

	Financial	Too many activities	Time w/family	Over Indulgence	Being alone	Memories
50%						
40%	40%	34%				37%
30%				28%	27%	
20%			17%			
10%						
0%						

Source: © copyright Mental Health America 2013

Top Holiday Stressors:

1. **Finances are the most common source of holiday stress** (40%). Parents are more stressed than all other demographic groups by finances (51%), and females (45%) are more likely than men to feel stressed by finances.

2. **37 percent of Americans feel stressed by memories of loved ones who passed away.** Latinos (50%) and African Americans (46%) are most stressed by these memories, compared to Non-Hispanic Whites (34%).

3. **Having too much to do causes stress for 34% of people during the holidays.** Parents are more stressed than any other demographic group by too much to do (43%).

Spending time with family is the *least* stressful activity. However, overall, Hispanics/Latinos (39%) and Native Americans (37%) experience greater stress from spending holidays with family than other demographic groups.

In-flight Checklist

Develop a holiday plan model. Do this as soon as possible—before the first holiday you will experience as a newlywed couple.

1) Make a list of the holidays each of you celebrates.

2) Prioritize your own list by rating each holiday's importance individually. Value any differences.

3) Prayerfully talk about how each of you desires to spend each holiday as a couple. How will you establish new traditions for each event?

4) Address possible conflicts with holiday traditions and plans for each of your families.

5) If possible, set up alternating years with each other's family.

6) Share the initial plan to each of your families. Be supportive of one another as a couple.

7) Be encouraged to establish your own traditions and share in special family events being sure to maintain a balance for you as a couple.

Holiday Planning Matrix					
Holiday	His Priority (1=Top, 2=Next, etc.)	Her Priority (1=Top, 2=Next, etc.)	Possible Family Conflicts? Who?	Year 1 Holiday Plan	Year 2 Holiday Plan
1)					
2)					
3)					
4)					
5)					
6)					

Source: Adapted from *The Solution for Marriages*[2]

Biblical References

Colossians 2:16-17 – *"Therefore do not let anyone judge you by what you eat or drink, or with regard to a religious festival, a New Moon celebration or a Sabbath day. These are a shadow of the things that were to come; the reality, however, is found in Christ."*

Chapter 11

Becoming Full-time Caregivers
For Your Parent(s)
Flying in the Historic Airplane

Pre-Flight Information

As the "Boomer" Generation matures so do the needs of family. Many will become grandparents! Some will share homes with offspring due to economic complications. Most challenging is becoming the full-time caregiver for one or both parents as they attain milestones in their lives as well. Many couples will elect to either join the elders in their homes or provide suitable quarters such as 'in-laws apartment' or other accommodations in their homes. Some will elect to have care provided by professional facilities.

Caring for aging parents can be demanding and complex at times, but it is equally an honor and privilege as well as a God-given responsibility for each family member. 1 Timothy 5:8 gives us insight to the obligation: *"Anyone who does not provide for their relatives, and especially for their own household, has denied the faith and is worse than an unbeliever."*

Some elderly parental care can be extremely difficult, sometimes even controlling and manipulative by the self-seeking elder parent to dictate the lives and activities of family members. Some may claim they are unable to perform even basic tasks such as pouring themselves a glass of water, when in reality they are fully capable physically and mentally, but choose to expect family members to cater to their every desire and urge.

The aging parent/child connection cannot, and must not, displace the relationship between husband and wife as first priority. The marriage vows spoken before God to "leave and cleave unto each other" should not be subject to needless stress and strain on the marital relationship due to the elder care. It is extremely important to understand the difference between caring for needs versus wants. Taking care of elderly parents can often lead the adult children to become enablers of their parents without realizing it. For example, turning down the bed at night or preparing their tooth brush in the morning enables, when the parent has the capacity and ability to perform these simple tasks.

Taking care of elderly parents can also put stress on marriages unless clear boundaries have been established that supports all siblings, children, and grandchildren. It is important and necessary to care for aging parents, but equally vital to care for the requirements of your own immediate family, such as the husband/wife relationship and that of any children.

We have experienced the care of their parents. We cared for Chuck's mom for her final 8 years and Mae's mom during her last 7 years. Caring for Chuck's mom came after the early death of his father in 1991 at age 66. Although in relatively good health, his mother (Audrey) needed Cardiac Care, Diabetes management and more. Chuck and Mae moved from their 2,300 square foot, 4-bedroom, and 3-bath cull de sac home to a 12' X 12' bedroom in her home. Chuck committed to his father before his death that he would care for his mother. She attained her goal of experiencing the Millennium, transitioning to Heaven on January 2, 2000. They moved Mae's mom (Millie)—GG for Great Grandma—into their home in 2005. Millie survived two husbands, a daughter and son-in-law and a five-year old great-granddaughter. Prior to living with Mae and Chuck, she suffered with osteoarthritis, osteoporosis and cataracts. She later experienced cardiac failure and a fractured hip and femur from a fall. She lived her final days in hospice until going Home on July 29, 2012.

Their first hand knowledge enables them to share a few non-textbook, non-clinical experiences. Undoubtedly, the most difficult time in parent/elder care is watching the slow, progressive deterioration of physical and mental capacities. Each day brings new challenges. Some days only prayer and tears can offer strength, while other days its laughter that brings joy and builds hope. Memories are constantly being created—some fond, others painful. The Lord supplies the blessing each day for us to continue the care, give back the shelter, and provide the needs until the time comes for them to enjoy eternity with Him. Amen!

What Does Scripture Say About Elderly Care? – *The Captain Turns on the Fasten Seat Belt Sign*

1 Timothy 5:4, known as the instruction for the Church regarding widows, gives insight how to care for the parent: *"But if a widow has children or grandchildren, these should learn first of all to put their religion into practice by caring for their own family and so repaying their parents and grandparents, for this is pleasing to God."* The chapter goes on to share cautions and warnings on how Satan will attempt to interfere with the efforts.

Common Stressors

Common stressors encountered during elder care:

1) *Physical Limitations*

   - Restricted mobility
   - Sight regression
   - Unable to dress/undress self
   - Difficulty eating/feeding self

2) *Reduced Mental Capacity*
   - Forgetfulness of simple tasks
   - Unable to remember names
   - Short or long-term memory challenges
   - Unsure of familiar places or surroundings
   - Temper tantrums

3) *Health Problems*
   - Chronic or acute health issues
   - Improper nutrition and fluid intake
   - Sleep habits vary

4) *Personal Hygiene*
   - Needs help bathing
   - Toddler-like behavior with simple sanitation practices
   - Toilet habits become difficult to manage

Tips on Elder Care – *The Flight Crew Demonstrates the Safety Equipment*

Adult children must often take on the responsibility of caregiver before they are completely aware of everything involved with caring for an aging parent. When this occurs, the adult children must seek answers, hopefully, before the need arises, to many questions. Sometimes involving other family members can be helpful or engage the assistance of professionals (accountants, attorneys, and doctors, financial planners) to assist in drafting the documentation, if not already in place. Below are some areas:

- Who is the primary caregiver designate?

- What role will other family members play in the care?

    o Can teenagers and younger family members help?

    o Who will supervise shopping, doctor visits, etc?

- Are local elder Day-Care programs available?

    o What is the cost?

    o How will transportation be provided?

- Seek local support groups for families with similar circumstances.

- Are there any signs that some help is needed now? What?

- Who has a list of assets and their value?

- Is there a will, a living will, medical directive, power of attorney? If so, where?

- What are the parent's wishes regarding when to issue or agree to a "Do Not Resuscitate" order, also known as a DNR?

- Location of birth certificates, Social Security card, marriage and/or divorce certificates, education and military records.

- What about a pension? What is the amount? Is it directly deposited? Where?

- Does the parent receive Social Security payments? How much? How is it deposited?

- List all bank accounts, CD's, safety deposit boxes, IRA's, stocks, etc? Where?

- What are the debts? Mortgages, credit cards, car payment?

- Is there adequate medical insurance? Long-term care insurance? Medicare? Medicaid? Prescription plan?

- Has anyone consulted with an elder-care attorney?

- Can the elderly parent live alone? Where?

- What about an independent living, assisted living facility, or a nursing home?

- What medications are being taken and in what dosage? By prescription or over the counter?

- Name and location of the primary care physician.

- Are there any prepaid funeral expenses? Prepaid burial plot? Are there any specific funeral arrangements desired?

- Is an obituary notice in the newspaper desired? How much does it cost? (Some newspapers offer this as a complimentary service, while others charge hundreds of dollars for a two-inch block of text).

- Is there a preferred funeral home? Should there be a viewing? Who will deliver the eulogy?

- Is cremation desired? Are there any specific wishes regarding the funeral service?

Healthy Ways of Controlling the Uncontrollable – *Emergency Responses to Regain Control of the Aircraft*

1) Identify ways that you can avoid last minute crises by improving your planning and being more proactive.

2) Ensure regularly scheduled visits to the primary care physician for care and advice.

   a. Be sure to take notes between visits that you can share with the provider concerning the habits, behaviors, and general condition of your loved one.

3) Use assertive communication skills with the elder person, but don't be mean or aggressive.

4) Can you find anything positive in the situation? If so, choose to focus on that part of the issue more.

Ways to Cope with Unchangeable Circumstances – *You're Not the Pilot – So Let Him Fly for You*

1) Realize that you can't control everything, so don't become obsessed with these issues.

2) Share your feelings with a close friend or pastor. The emotional release can do you good.

3) Start an exercise and nutrition program and get more rest.

4) Treat yourself to something special (a short trip, perhaps) as a way to get away and emotionally regroup.

5) Find something you enjoy and do it at least once a day. Look forward to that special time each day.

6) Try to maintain your sense of humor.

7) Practice relaxation techniques when you encounter extra stress.

If you continue having difficulty in this area, consider engaging the assistance of a professional health care provider.

Before Take-off

1) What approach can you take to begin talking about elder care? What about situations you can't change?

2) How stressful is your daily life typically—apart from adding the parent care?

3) What are a few ideas to help cope with the stress of elder care?

In-Flight Exercises

Caring for your parent(s) can create an emotional and/or physical drain for you. Some days you will wonder how you will find mental and physical strength to continue providing the care. Other times you'll take a deep breath and say to yourself, "Wow, I can't believe how blessed I am to care for my mom." What is important is to be able to properly deal with the various situations as they surface. Most importantly, keep yourself in the best possible physical health. Seek the care of your own doctor to ensure you maintain proper care of your needs.

Stress is often managed using a prioritization process. Develop a list to identify the important issues you are each facing.

1) For each item on your list, determine which situations can be changed or resolved and which ones are outside of your control.

2) Prioritize the ones you can control and want to work on.

3) Discuss ways that you can better cope with the issues that can't be changed or are beyond your control.

Biblical References

Proverbs 23:22 – *"Listen to your father, who gave you life, and do not despise your mother when she is old."*

Deuteronomy 5:16 – *"Honor your father and your mother, as the LORD your God has commanded you, so that you may live long and that it may go well with you in the land the LORD your God is giving you."*

Chapter 12

Joy and Sadness

Pre-flight Information

This chapter demonstrates the strength of the Holy Spirit when we open our hearts and allow Him to work. Many couples experience the hardship of a miscarriage, losing a child, a pet, or a grandchild. In many cases, they feel they have 'no place to go' for assistance in the grief process. The opposite is actually very true. Several excellent international programs, licensed professionals, local churches, hospice programs, and the love from others who have experienced the same loss are available. Seeking the best support path is often very difficult for some and may take many weeks, months or years to heal. Every loss is unique and special because the depth of the loss is simply the level of love we have for the one we lose.

Our hope is you'll use the information shared by these couples to draw strength should you be challenged with similar experiences. Know that God is our creator and healer.

We experienced the loss of our first child in 1971 by miscarriage while stationed in California. They felt alone, lost, and alienated. Geographically separated from family and friends, they turned to God and their local pastor. Mae's mom and sister came for short visits, helping to comfort and offer support. Not having the well thought-out support of programs such as today's Grief Share, they 'stuffed' the loss and continued with life. In January of 1972, they were blessed by the birth of their son and in 1977, a daughter. Then, on Labor Day weekend, 2010, they experienced the death of 5-year old Amber, their grand-daughter, after a short battle with Osteosarcoma.

The Dettman's were surrounded by many people who offered prayer, comfort, and support, but this loss led them on a journey much different than before. Both sought the strength of God by 'leaning into Him' versus running away. Not surprisingly, their church hosts a world-renown program – Grief Share. Mae attended first and then Chuck joined her a couple weeks later. The series of lessons gave them tools to understand how grief is not something we put in a box; it cannot be set to a timetable, and most of all, how grief is dealt with is very special for each person. God brought about healing for the miscarriage 39-years prior, taught us how to share our losses (his best friend, his parents and her father, step-father, half-sister, and now Amber for both of us) plus the significance of each loss. They went on to co-facilitate the program until the death of Mae's mom in July 2012. They're using the tools they learned and now teach others how to experience grief properly.

Rainer and Kerstin Knaack have been married since 2005 and have overcome a number of challenges, including three miscarriages and a stillbirth in the ninth month of pregnancy. They know firsthand what it is like when a couple experiences joy and sadness during their marriage. Their experience speaks a true passion for couples who encounter various challenges in life. By discovering their destination, the two decided in 2012 to withdraw from their careers.

The Knaacks combine their firm Christian faith with excellent training skills and a passion to serve other couples. Kerstin's desire is to train managers, pastors, and counselors and lay couples. The two desire to personally invest locally and internationally as marriage mentors.

After six years of work at Siemens Healthcare, Rainer devoted his life entirely to the development of an international marriage mentoring program to specifically, and professionally, strengthen marriages, families and relationships. He holds two graduate degrees: Master of Business Administration at the University of Cooperative Education and Design Studies at the University of Arts in Berlin. After he finished his fellowship at Edith Cowan University in Perth, Australia, his second thesis, "Decisive Leadership by Tacit Knowledge," was published as a book.

Kerstin first studied dance, singing, and acting within the scope of music in Berlin and is a qualified foreign language assistant. She was employed by a company that offers Business Theater as a training method, linking her professional background in art and business. Later, she transitioned to an international company with a focus on staff and led a team of seven internal and 200 external workers. She also trained the trainers from the company. Kerstin is a Certified Business Coach and BDVT DISC ® trainer.

Rainer and Kerstin Knaack are certified as marriage mentors and Seminar Directors by PREPARE/ENRICH. They became certified as *The Solution for Marriages* Mentor Trainers in June 2012. They returned to Surrey/Vancouver, Canada, to begin a first ever Marriage Ministry at Relate Church under the tutelage of Pastors John and Helen Burns. Now, at home in Konstanz, Germany, they are training Marriage Mentor Couples at their home church, Hillsong Church Germany, and internationally. For more on the Knaacks and their ministry, visit http://www.RelateWorks.com.

Below are the testimonies of Rainer and Kerstin as they released their most precious to the Lord. Rainer and Kerstin share their journey and grieving process.

One week after our daughter Loah's birth - "Love letter for being able to share with God and people whilst grieving".

Dear Loah,

On Wednesday, 30 March 2011, shortly before 5 pm you got real: we were honoured to welcoming you, dear Loah, as our new family member with all our love and affection at Lake Constance, Germany.

Due to your premature birth, you just weighed about 1,17 kg and you started 39 cm tall. Overall, the sad-beautiful aspect of this occurrence is that you have already fallen asleep within the womb and directly took the "short-cut" to our beloved creator.

Dearest Loah, we are incredibly proud and privileged of being your earthly parents. Since 3 September 2010, we have been loving you from the first minute of your existence. Together, we are astonished by your peaceful charisma, your unique character and your complete and ravishing beauty. As our treasure in Heaven, you have to know and keep in mind how wonderful our souls are effected, changed and enlightened by your aura.

We are filled with inner peace by sensing your presence from eternity and guidance in this world. In deepest, parental love.

Your mummy Kerstin and daddy Rainer with Frederike, Joanna and Freimut, Lili and Dieter, all praying brothers and sisters.

P.S.

There are two things calming our hearts since you have been born:

> *a) One of our favorite books "The Shack", last 7 pages of chapter 11[1].*

> *b) Scott Wilson's Word from 27 March 2011[2].*

About 9 months after:

"Written review after the first months of grieving to find out how to be a blessing and help for others."

~Kerstin Knaack~

SheLoves.com on February 15, 2012[3]

Wellness Wednesday: Why Hide? My Journey of Hope, Faith and Overcoming

"If I don't share my life and the difficult journey I have made, it will be harder for God to work through me."

~Kerstin Knaack~

I am ten weeks pregnant. It takes courage for me to tell you that.

Why? This is my fourth pregnancy—my first three babies are in heaven.

I am from Germany. There, we don't usually tell people we are pregnant until the fourth month of pregnancy. But several weeks ago, I went to Brazil and found out the women there announce their pregnancies as soon as they have a positive test in their hands. I asked why they do this, considering most miscarriages occur within the first three months. They said that in their culture, they celebrate and mourn together. If something happens to the baby, they come to the mother's side, offering everything from a big hug to cooking for her or massaging her feet. Whatever she needs, they journey with her.

Loss

My first miscarriage was in 2009 in the eighth week; the second was in 2011 in the 33rd week and the third was at the end of 2011 in the 12th week. All these losses were difficult, but to give birth to a dead baby in the ninth month of pregnancy was definitely the most painful.

After the third miscarriage, I wasn't able to pray or worship. My heart ached, but I had good friends who carried me through. When I was far from God, they spoke life and truth over me. My church gathered around and carried me. When I couldn't pray, they prayed for me; when I couldn't worship, they worshiped for me.

I knew that death doesn't come from God — He is love and nothing bad comes from him—but He did allow this to happen.

Restoration

After several weeks, I reached a place where I was able to think about my situation in a different way. If God allowed this to happen, there must be something good within these situations. This was a turning point for me—I wanted to turn bad into good. It was a decision, not a feeling. I chose to no longer accept being bound by lies.

So many good things happened as a result of my miscarriages:

- my marriage to my husband Rainer became stronger and we decided to give 100 percent of our lives to God, stepping into His purpose for us

- the opportunity developed to do an internship at Relate Church, Canada, with Pastors John and Helen Burns

- my father returned to my life after 28 years of rejection

- friends put their lives into Jesus' hands.

Overcoming

From now on, I will no longer hide. *I have discovered that it is healthy for me to talk about how I feel and which thoughts and emotions have kept me away from God. If I don't share my life and the difficult journey I have made, it will be harder for God to work through me. I want Him to use me to help other women and to fulfill His plan.*

That's why I am openly telling people that I am pregnant for the fourth time.

Is it easy for me to enjoy my pregnancy? Definitely not. Every day I am reminded of the past, the positive pregnancy tests; pictures of my big belly; the ultrasounds; the decorated nursery; the movements in my belly; memories of the day I was told our daughter had passed away; the pain of giving birth to a dead baby and the joy of having her in our arms; Rainer's love letter to our new daughter; the invoice from the funeral parlor.

Stepping Forward in Faith

How do I deal with these images and the daily fear of possibly having the same pain again? *There is no magic solution–it's a journey every day. I think back to those Brazilian women, who understand what sisterhood means and I know that if I fall, my sisterhood will carry me. And I talk about it. If I am overwhelmed by fear, I ask my husband or a friend to help me.*

"The opposite of fear is faith. God holds my life in His hands. I trust Him."

Since the loss of Loah, the Knaacks are the proud parents to a strong, healthy, and wonderful gift of God. Noah was born May 5th, 2013.

Rainer and Kerstin Knaack are the German translators of our first book, *The Solution for Marriages.* So many times, we draw from their strength and discernment. We cherish their love and friendship beyond imagination.

Biblical References

Matthew 5:4 – *"Blessed are those who mourn, for they will be comforted."*

Psalm 147:3 – *"He heals the brokenhearted and binds up their wounds."*

John 16:33 – *"I have told you these things, so that in me you may have peace. In this world you will have trouble. But take heart! I have overcome the world."*

2 Corinthians 1:3-7 – *" Praise be to the God and Father of our Lord Jesus Christ, the Father of compassion and the God of all comfort, who comforts us in all our troubles, so that we can comfort those in any trouble with the comfort we ourselves receive from God. For just as we share abundantly in the sufferings of Christ, so also our comfort abounds through Christ. If we are distressed, it is for your comfort and salvation; if we are comforted, it is for your comfort, which produces in you patient endurance of the same sufferings we suffer. And our hope for you is firm, because we know that just as you share in our sufferings, so also you share in our comfort."*

Recommended Resources

Young, William P. *The Shack: Reflections for Every Day of the Year*. Newbury Park, CA: Windblown Media, 2012.

Chapter 13

Intimacy in Marriage
Enjoy the Flight – God's Way!

"Do not deprive each other except perhaps by mutual consent and for a time, so that you may devote yourselves to prayer. Then come together again so that Satan will not tempt you because of your lack of self-control."

~ 1 Corinthians 7:5 ~

Early Christian Perceptions of Sex[1]- *Abort the Flight, No Fun on This Journey!*

Much of church history has projected sex as distasteful, evil, or only for reproduction. Many non-Christian cultures and religions have distorted what God intended for sexual enjoyment as well. Through the worldly persuasion of Greek culture (e.g. Plato), the early church saw sex and passion as basically evil. Some examples of this are:

1) Tertullian – An early Christian pastor (AD 160-220) and Ambrose (4th century) who favored ending the human race rather than continuing sexual activity.

2) Origen (AD 185 – 254) believed sex was so wicked that he symbolically fictionalized the Song of Solomon and emasculated himself so he would never enjoy sexual pleasure.

3) Crisostamin (4th century) stated Adam and Eve failed to have sexual relations until the Fall, and therefore sex is caused by sin.

In our 21st Century fast paced, busy lifestyles, we sometimes forget one of the greatest blessings given to us by God. As schedules become complex and populated with 'busy things,' we often do not find time to be intimate with our spouse. Intimacy is usually thought of as 'sexual intimacy.' However, that is only one element of intimacy. The truly intimate couple recognizes all the elements:

- Spiritual intimacy - the intensity of devotion

  - Emotional intimacy - the thrill of romance

  - Intellectual intimacy - the honing of mind

  - Sexual intimacy - the physical bliss

Spiritual Intimacy - Spiritual intimacy is often not easy to achieve, but is in fact the most significant form of closeness since it profoundly influences the other areas. Countless couples find it difficult to achieve, because it is really trinity in nature — imminence among three: husband, wife, and God!

Emotional Intimacy - A soul-mate union is the expression that often defines emotional intimacy. It describes a profound attachment between husband and wife, sometimes referred to as love chatter. Some people like to make a distinction between the two by assuming emotional intimacy is learned while a link between soul-mates is automatic — intended and crafted in Heaven.

Intellectual Intimacy - Most couples don't comprehend the significance of intellectual intimacy in their relationship, but it is a fundamental factor to the overall sense of closeness. The more we can learn of God's design for the fulfillment and enjoyment of total intimacy, the greater satisfaction we'll experience in the relationship.

Sexual Intimacy - Sexual intimacy in marriage is vital to a strong, joyful, and healthy relationship between husband and wife. Joined with the emotional, intellectual, and spiritual expressions, God intended husband and wife to take pleasure in the experience of sexual intimacy in marriage. Intimacy is the final human experience!

The Bible is the ultimate source of sexual relationship advice in a Christian marriage. Here, in the Bible, we discover educational advice and real life examples relating to sex and marriage, passion, lust, and intimacy. This centuries old "how to" manual shares information about such modern topics as how to achieve intimate passion, how to please your husband or wife, and how to solve the problem of men and romance!

Many people have a distorted perception about how much Christian marriage advice is in the Bible, together with what the Bible says about sex. We fail to remember that this whole intimacy and sex thing is God's idea! Why question His authority and plan?

Our sex drive is one of the most powerful forces God gifted us to experience. Envision this drive being out of control, like a raging lion. It is injurious and destructive. The Bible gives accounts of the entire sexual experience spectrums. Examples of people exercising out-of-control sex destroyed nations (Sodom and Gomorrah, Genesis 19) are discussed along with God's blueprint, the highlight of sexual experiences found in the Song of Solomon.

Scores of biblical and poetic references to sexuality and lovemaking originate in the Bible. Proverbs 5:15-19 teaches the hazard of promiscuity as contrasted with the beauty of sex in marriage:

"Drink water from your own cistern, running water from your own well. Should your springs overflow in the streets, your streams of water in the public squares? Let them be yours alone, never to be shared with strangers. May your fountain be blessed, and may you rejoice in the wife of your youth. A loving doe, a graceful deer—may her breasts satisfy you always, may you ever be intoxicated with her love."

Okay, so answer the question, "What sexual practices are okay?" There may be a lot of diverse Christian perceptions on sex, but God gives us strong and healthy principles to follow.

We must be cautious to distinguish the difference between what the Bible actually says about sex and what our background and rearing may instruct us.

How Do We Know What's Okay? – *Pre-flight Checklist Complete;*
Ready for Take-off!

"Wouldn't it be nice to have a list of sexual practices categorized by
'sinful' or 'okay'? Is there such a list? Would everyone agree with the
list? Is there a solution to this dilemma? We think the answers to those
questions are: yes, no, no, and probably not—in that order." – Melissa
and Louis McBurney, M.D[2]

When I say there are countless Christian viewpoints on biblically
acceptable sex and sexual practices,   I'm understating the magnitude
of diversity! Taking the above quote seriously, we will not find an
absolute list! However, we will find:

  ▪ **Instructions** from His Word—we'll call them the **Thou**
    Shalt Nots.

  ▪ **Values** that are commonly accepted in their purpose and
    practiced by couples to aid them in discerning their
    Christian views on sex.

1. **Thou Shalt Nots:**

   Christian beliefs on sex must be grounded on biblical teaching.
   The Bible is very clear-cut on the subject of certain exclusions
   that, if followed, place a clear hedge of defense around the
   married couple and the holiness of God's propose for sexuality
   between a husband and wife. Here are a few examples:

   God unmistakably forbids infidelity (engaging in sex with
   anyone other than your spouse), calling it sin. Additionally, the
   Bible prohibits fornication (having casual sex frequently with
   different partners or of being indiscriminate in the choice of
   sexual partners), naming it as sinful as well. God's exclusions
   are not intended as restrictions to our freedom; they are designed
   as shields to our well being. Grabbing a child about to run into
   oncoming traffic is not considered limiting the child's behavior;
   it's simply a parental responsibility to protect the child from
   harm! It is so with God's "Thou Shalt Nots." His directions

protect us from many moral, physical, and emotional dangers.

In Matthew 5, 6, and 7 (The Sermon on the Mount), Jesus teaches on how the behaviors like adultery or fornication begin by an inner stimulus of our heart. He then demonstrates how lustful feelings about a female, who is not your wife, constituted adultery from God's perspective! Our Christian perception on sex is not founded on civic opinion, but on God's Word.

Sinful acts such as homosexuality, bestiality, and incest are listed in Scripture (Leviticus 18, Romans 1:21-32, 1 Thessalonians 4:1-8, and a Corinthians 6:12-20).

2. **The One and Only Principle:**

This phrase explains the sanctified covenant between a husband and wife that establishes the foundation of their relationship. When we say, "You are my one and only love," you are establishing faith and assurance. Intimacy (all four types) is the element that guarantees sexual happiness. However, this cannot be assured unless a high level of dedication is devoted in the marriage. Disloyalty of any kind erases this key component. Essentially, the Christian viewpoint on sex can be summarized as one man and one woman for life!

3. **The Back to Basics Principle:**

The principle of God's design for the physiology of sex is Back to Basics. Husbands and wives are to enjoy one another sexually! Ever check the anatomical differences between a man and woman? God created us distinctly for the union and the pleasure that accompanies that connection. Regardless of the practices enjoyed by the couple, the Back to Basics Principle should remind us of the intent and fulfillment God had in mind.

4. **The Hooked on You Principle:**

"I'm hooked on you," is an attitude that forces out any form of sexuality or sensuality not straightforwardly focused in the direction of your spouse. Sex is the connectivity that bonds a husband and wife to each other. Everything done or seen that draws attention away from one another or creates a dependency on anything except your spouse must be removed from your marriage! Today we are bombarded with pornography, metaphors of inappropriate sexual behaviors, internet, social media, fetishes, fantasies, or illusions that can become addictive and draw couples apart.

5. **The Good for Both Principle:**

Any activity in the sexual relationship must be "good for both" spouses. 1 Thessalonians 4:3-5 gives direction stating, *"It is God's will that you should be sanctified: that you should avoid sexual immorality; that each of you should learn to control your own body in a way that is holy and honorable, not in passionate lust like the pagans, who do not know God."* For example, if either spouse wants to try something different during their lovemaking, but the idea isn't pleasurable to the other, then the request should be dropped.

Seeking marriage advice from a counselor is sometimes a necessary path in a marriage. Be sure your counselor provides biblical marriage counseling. Interview the counselor to be sure they provide Christian marriage advice based on God's wisdom found in the Bible. Adhering to God's design for marriage and intimacy produces magnificent outcomes for a long lasting, healthy, and strong marriage!

Biblical marriage counseling, different than other types of counseling, is the simple application of the standards and philosophy taught in the Bible for marriages. Christian marriage counsel, then, begins with essential truths. A few are listed below:

o   Marriage is a covenant, not a contract, designed by God (Hosea 2:19)

- o Restoration of broken marriages is the goal (Malachi 2:13-16)

- o The husband seeks to meet all the needs of his wife and the wife seeks to meet all the needs of the husband (Eph 5:25-33)

- o The Bible is the decisive authority on strong relationships—especially within the marriage (Genesis 2:24)

- o The biblical model for both a husband and a wife is to surrender in order to pursue the well-being, joy, and happiness of their spouse (Philippians 2:2-4)

In-flight Exercises

The questions below are designed to open a dialog for couples. Many times engaged and married couples expect their spouse to be educated and prepared for a fulfilling sexual rapport in marriage. Nothing could be further from the truth! Most have heard *much* about sex, but few envision it in a manner that *equally* honors the creator of sex (God) and that sex was created for (a husband and wife).

- I am content chatting with my spouse about sexual topics.

- I am entirely fulfilled with the amount of fondness my spouse gives me.

- I am troubled about my spouse's past sexual actions.

- I am disturbed that my partner's importance of sex might be unlike mine.

- My spouse and I speak plainly about our sexual outlook.

- My partner, from time to time, utilizes or refuses intimacy unfairly.

- I am unwilling to be affectionate with my husband/wife because he/she regularly construes it as a sexual advance.

- We have discussed and agreed on the restrictions of our premarital sexual activity.

Biblical References

Hebrews 13:4 – *"Marriage should be honored by all, and the marriage bed kept pure, for God will judge the adulterer and all the sexually immoral."*

1 Corinthians 6:18-20 - *"Flee from sexual immorality. All other sins a person commits are outside the body, but whoever sins sexually, sins against their own body. Do you not know that your bodies are temples of the Holy Spirit, who is in you, whom you have received from God? You are not your own; you were bought at a price. Therefore honor God with your bodies."*

Genesis 1:28 - *"God blessed them and said to them, "Be fruitful and increase in number; fill the earth and subdue it. Rule over the fish in the sea and the birds in the sky and over every living creature that moves on the ground."*

Genesis 2:24 - *"That is why a man leaves his father and mother and is united to his wife, and they become one flesh."*

Recommended Resources

Dillow, Joseph C. *Solomon on Sex.* New York, NY: Thomas Nelson, 1977.

Gardner, Tim Alan. *Sacred Sex.* Colorado Springs, CO: WaterBrook Press, 2002.

LaHaye, Tim F., and Beverly LaHaye. *The Act of Marriage: the Beauty of Sexual Love.* Grand Rapids: Zondervan Pub. House, 1976.

Penner, Clifford, and Joyce Penner. *Getting Your Sex Life off to a Great Start: a Guide for Engaged and Newlywed Couples.* Dallas: Word Pub., 1994.

Chapter 14

Handling Cultural Differences[1]
This Radar Takes Direction-finding Awareness!

Pre-Flight Information

In America today, more people are marrying someone from a different religion or racial/ethnic group than ever before. According to the Pew Forum on Religion and Public Life, nearly 37% of Americans are married to someone of a different faith.[2]

Additionally, the 2010 U.S. Census reported that 10% of Americans are married to someone of a different race.[3] Researchers have offered several possible explanations for these growing trends:

Couples are more likely to marry outside of their faith when these contributing factors are in play:

1) They have a common religious orientation, education level, or global perspective. They are more independent of their family, do not feel a need to be of the same faith as their parents, experience a divorce, or expect a more balanced division of household responsibilities.[4]
2) Diverse immigrants provide local residents knowledge about and exposure to religious difference and build acceptance of other religions in American society.[5]

Interracial couples are more likely to marry when these contributing factors are in play:

1) They have a common religious orientation, education level, or global perspective.
2) Racial boundaries weaken, differences narrow, and language and residential barriers diminish, thus making intermarriage more likely to occur.
3) Immigrants of the third generation or later have become more comfortable with the local language and culture.[6, 7]

Intermarriage can benefit immigrants or ethnic minorities to become part of the dominate culture, though they may lose identification with their own.[8]

To appreciate the specific cultural issues a multicultural couple may potentially endure, they should take into consideration such concerns as socio-economic standing, faith or creed, age, cultural persuasion, and value systems.

Couples in multicultural or multiracial relationships usually have above average curiosity and excitement to learn about the others' ancestry and traditions. Although this excitement and eagerness presents new awareness, these marriages also come with greater challenges in building a lasting and fulfilled marriage.

Navigational Challenges in Cultural Divergence

Every couple needs to build and use strong communication and conflict resolution skills to beneficially manage the hard times when they come.

The items below are by no means exhaustive, but simply a sample of a few common challenges couples my face in a multicultural marriage.

1) Language differences cultivate communication challenges.

2) Different desires in levels of harmony or intimacy between partners.

3) Role expectations, including the extended family, and the resolution of these concerns.

4) Birthdays, anniversaries, celebrations, and holidays (how to celebrate—his, hers or both).

5) What about the food to be served in the home?

6) Where will the couple live (the neighborhood, housing expectations, possible prejudices)?

7) How will the couple maintain their social and cultural friendships as a couple and individually?

8) Cultural identity – how does the couple plan to maintain their unique cultural identity while blending a new 'couple identity'?

The scale of impact these and other issues have on the marriage will largely depend on how the cultural groups accept and adopt the viewpoint and way of life of the other. The couple may do well, but the extended family, friends, and communities may not perceive and behave with the same level of acceptance and adoption. The couple may be subject to unmerited discrimination, their children possibly ridiculed, and more.

Visual Flight Rules for Cultural Differences

Prospective Benefits from Cultural Differences

1) **Embrace the opportunity.**

   Don't only look at the negative aspects of marriages between people from different backgrounds and cultures. Instead appreciate the differences. Understand and respect each other's differences.

2) **Learn more about the culture.**

   Surprisingly, many multicultural couples fail to chat about the imagery or significance of each other's important cultural traditions. Knowing the importance of these traditions will help you, not only to understand them, but it can also aid in identifying yourself with some of them. Appreciate the fact that this will help you accept and embrace the culture of your spouse.

3) **Overcome challenges.**

   Different languages, customs, qualities, or problems will arise. Every marriage has one or more of these tribulations that need to be conquered each day. If you are in a relationship with someone raised in a similar type of home or even a similar culture you will still have problems just as if they were from a completely different ethnicity or speak a different language.

4) **Bilingual children.**

In some families the parents come from a different country. Their children will naturally grow up bilingual. Do the work and spend the time to persuade your kids to learn the native language of their parents as well the traditions of that culture. The children and you will benefit socially and possibly professionally.

5) **Help your "*foreign*" spouse feel at home.**

Visit the family and places your spouse will feel at home with. These places are either cultural or reminders of their home. Assist your spouse in developing friendships with people from his or her country or families that speak their language.

6) **Maintain contact with family.**

It is essential that your "foreign" spouse maintains contact with his or her family. Don't allow the distance of time to present thoughts yearning for family, homesickness, and even possible loneliness. Today, the Internet and tools like Facebook and Skype make contact much easier and your spouse happier.

7) **When possible, travel together.**

One advantage of being married to someone from another country is that you get to travel from time to time. When you can travel, make sure to visit your spouse's family and learn about their culture firsthand.

8) **Legality and staying in one country.**

It matters not if you live in your home country and your spouse is a foreigner or vice versa; you and your spouse must become legal in that country. You must follow the immigration laws. Find the Consulate and the Department of Immigration in your state or province as quickly as possible. Be sure to consider the financial aspects of obtaining residency. You should discuss this in great detail before your relationship becomes more serious.

Keeping Differences from Causing Disconnection

1) **Understand and Explore**

Intercultural marriages offer the prospect of expanding an in-depth admiration of other ways of life. Rejoice in the celebrations distinctive to your partner's homeland or religious tradition. Spend time getting to know his/her family. Enjoy the foods native to your partner's country. Enthusiasm that values your partner's culture displays love and respect.

2) **Respect Differences**

Genuine cultural diversity exists and should not be taken lightly. However, neither should these differences be perceived out of context. When differing viewpoints take place, seek to understand, rather than to judge.

3) **Look for Commonalities**

It is important to be conscious of different cultures and to look for commonalities. Look for comparable ideals, preferences, and interests. Sharing certain core principles (such as truthfulness, work ethic, charity, etc.) can diminish stress in your marriage.

4) **Keep What Matters Most to You**

Understanding your mate's culture is important. However, you mustn't give in to pressure to discard treasured portions of your own traditions. Intercultural marriages require give and take, but they should not force one person to throw out central parts of his/her uniqueness.

5) **Don't Make Assumptions**

Don't let cultural stereotypes dictate your understanding of your partner. Instead, let your own knowledge of your partner (his/her persona and view) form your perception. Furthermore, some expression of your partner's cultural characteristics may be more (or less) significant to him/her, so find out what is most significant to your partner. Carefully talk about any expectations for the relationship and/or marriage that may be influenced by your upbringing. These areas may include thoughts on gender roles, intimacy (see chapter 12), finances (be sure to study chapter 6) and the holidays.

6) **Be Patient**

Our civilization is by and large more tolerant of intercultural relationships, but many families still object, especially in the outset of the relationship. However, most families become more accepting with the passage of time. Often, apprehension about intercultural (and in particular, interracial) relationships are embedded in terms of the impact on any future children. While, even today, multiracial children may still encounter certain challenges, the American Academy of Child and Adolescent Psychiatry notes that such children are likely to celebrate diversity and appreciate being raised with the benefit of varied cultures. Should you initially encounter resistance from your family, try not to be too reactionary. Instead, patiently affirm your family of your respect for your partner and the special values in him or her. Hopefully, they will grow to love your partner as much as you do.

7) **Plan for the Future**

Cultural differences often become more sensitive when couples plan to marry or have children. Our culture is part of our worldview—and our worldview influences how we see everything, including relationships. Loving your partner means loving him/her for who he or she is and culture is a distinct part of that. While cultural differences can introduce certain challenges, these challenges are certainly manageable within the context of respectful and supportive relationships.

Prospective Areas of Cultural Difference and Conflict

Is Your Relationship Healthy?

A healthy relationship is described by a feeling of commitment, contentment, and safety. Ask yourself if your relationship has the following traits:

1) **Good Communication**

Good communication is the means to all relationships. When you communicate your feelings, wants, and goals, you express who you are now and your hope for your future. You learn in the same way from your partner. Creating a transparent tone of communication allows you to cultivate a closer and equipped future together.

2) **Commitment**

Commitment is essential to a strong, lasting and healthy relationship. It means you can depend on each other and chart for a future together. A strong, committed relationship gives you pleasure in the good times and gets you through the bad times.

3) **Trust**

Feeling at ease in a marriage is a consequence of trust. When you trust your spouse to treat you well and to speak in truth, thoughts of suspicion and resentment are tossed aside in favor of love and honesty. You have the assurance of knowing your spouse is attentive of your best interest. Trust is an element of friendship, an important aspect of a healthy marriage.

4) **Fairness and Respect**

Give-and-take in marriages is so important. Do you both have a say in your leisure activities, which friends to hang out with, the length of time to spend with relatives, and major purchases? Your relationship is not a tug-of-war, but rather a shared reverence and healthy compromise. Sound like your marriage? Good! A healthy attachment is designed to enhance the lives of the people involved, making them more contented and more satisfied.

Is Your Relationship Unhealthy?

A marriage is unwholesome if it involves disrespectful, mean, abusive, controlling, or violent behavior. Couples do not start with a bad relationship, but they do happen. Maybe you don't trust your spouse, or maybe you can't tell him/her how you honestly feel, or you're afraid of him/her. If this rings true for you, you should consider seeking the help of your pastor, or a Christian professional counselor.

Here are some signs that your relationship may be doing more harm than good:

1) **Disrespect**

Someone who loves you will not insult or demean you, even if they claim to be doing it *"for your own good."* When you respect someone, you appreciate them and accept them for who they are. A respectful relationship allows spouses to have different opinions.

2) **Jealousy**

Like a steak knife, jealousy stabs away at a marriage until little else remains but fear, anxiety and mistrust. Jealousy builds resentment, instills suspicion and festers until the marriage is in crisis. It is normal to be a bit envious now and then. However, your spouse should not make you feel guilty about a new job, spending time with friends, or your success.

3) **Abuse and Violence**

Nearly every couple argues, and you may get quite angry with each other, but healthy relationships do not include abuse or violence as part of these disagreements. Important warning signs of verbal, emotional, and physical abuse include:

- Insults, demeaning language, and constant put-downs.
- Physical abuse (hitting, shoving, or slapping).
- Forced sexual activity.

If abuse or violence is a part of your life as a couple, you should seek professional assistance. No one deserves to be abused or made to do something that makes them uncomfortable. If you are experiencing any of these things in your relationship, call the National Domestic Violence Hotline at 1-800-799-7233 (SAFE) for help.

Being in a healthy relationship is a great part of life! Relationships give people the chance to share their experiences and complement their lives. But healthy relationships take work. Both partners need to remain committed and make an effort to keep the love and respect alive.

Ultimately, the strength of a marriage depends most on the two people involved, not the two cultures.

Cultural Differences Summary

Racial Differences/Similarities and Marital Happiness

Couples of different racial and ethnic backgrounds tend to view their differences primarily as cultural rather than racial, with the exception of when they were initially attracted to their partner or if they had experienced incidences involving prejudice or discrimination.[9] Being of different races can definitely pose a challenge for intercultural couples. These challenges can definitely be overcome. However, if couples face disapproval and social pressure from families and society, their relationships may become highly stressful as a result.

Further, stress experienced in intercultural marriages may also be related to childrearing, time orientation, gender role expectations, connections to extended family, and particularly, which family subsystem will take priority or be dominant.[10]

Not all intercultural marriages are stressful and divorce prone. However, research indicates that interracial marriages were 13% more likely, in one report, to divorce than same-race marriages.[11] Though interracial marriage did not predict divorce per se, they were generally less stable and the risks varied by ethnicity. Among Whites, the ethnic group least likely to participate in interracial marriage, women tended to report the most stress. Among Native Americans, the ethnic group most likely to be involved in an interracial marriage (at over 50%), the distress rate was about twice as high as it was for Native Americans who were not involved in an intermarriage. The distress rate for Hispanics was elevated only when they married non-Whites, reaching over twice the rate of those married homogamously to other Hispanics. Interestingly, studies have found that if intermarriage improved the socioeconomic status of Hispanics or White women, the distress rate decreased.

Intermarriages involving African Americans were the least stable (especially with a White wife).[12 13] Rates of distress also increased among Hispanics and Native Americans who intermarried. Intermarriage among Asians did not elicit increased distress for any groups, which may be a result of the fact that they are among the most integrated minority group in American society.[14] In fact, marriages with an Asian partner were generally more stable than White homogamous marriages. Interestingly, the success of all of the marriages, except Asian–White, was predicted by the most divorce-prone group represented in the couple, rather than a balance of the two. The Asian–White couple's risk of divorce was a result of the balance of the two groups.[15]

Couples who overcome these challenges are more likely to focus on their similarities and perceive differences as strengths that broaden their view and enrich their relationship. They carefully discuss and negotiate the expectations and possible repercussions of conflicting cultures. Strengths in these relationships arise from spousal support, trust, and belief in each other. Immersion in either's culture can bring a unique sensitivity and awareness of differences, but also broaden their worldview.[16]

While marrying someone from a different culture or religion can provide some unique challenges, it can also provide some beautiful and enriching growing opportunities.

In-Flight Exercises[17]

Here are a number of things intercultural couples can do to reinforce their relationship.

When it comes to love, relationships can be like cars: constant care and adjustment (instead of pricey and painful visits to the body shop/marriage counselor) are often the best way to improve and strengthen your bond.

1) *"Stop all shame, blame, and criticism. Instead ask for what you want in a clear, specific, and positive manner, and express appreciation for your partner. To elaborate: Men need to feel competent—that they make a contribution and that it is noticed. They like to be told what 'behavior' makes you happy. Since men tend to express affection by doing things, you should interpret their actions as love. When men know what to do and are acknowledged for it, they tend to keep doing it."* — Harville Hendrix, PhD, author of *Getting the Love You Want*

2) *"Change from a critical habit of mind, in which you're very involved with your partner's mistakes, to a positive one, in which you catch him doing something right. Notice one small thing, and express genuine appreciation. That will change your interaction patterns from escalating negativity and criticism to building a culture of appreciation."* — John M. Gottman, PhD, author of *The Relationship Cure: A 5 Step Guide to Strengthening Your Marriage, Family, and Friendships*

3) *"When your relationship starts to break down, you need AAA: an Apology, Affection, and a promise of Action. You say you're sorry for what you've said or done to hurt or disappoint your partner. You immediately offer a hug, a kiss—some meaningful gesture of warmth. You pledge to do something that matters to your partner ('From now on, I will...'). And, of course, you stick to that. This whole AAA thing can take two minutes, but in that time you've healed the past, built a bridge to the present, and created hope for your future."* — Mira Kirshenbaum, psychotherapist and author of *The Weekend Marriage*

4) *"With books on the market like How to Make Love Like a Porn Star, one of the greatest services you can do for a guy is to reassure him that he doesn't have to make love like a porn star. You can show him how to have sex like a woman: creative, sensual, non-genital-based, and more pleasure-than orgasm-focused. Lead him to an experience that goes beyond his penis and makes him fully engaged—mind, body, and soul."* — Ian Kerner, PhD, author of *She Comes First*

5) *"All relationships grow a bit stale as time goes by, and the longer-lasting they are, the staler they can get. The best thing you can do is pump in some fresh air. A long weekend in a romantic hideaway would be ideal, but even a few hours in a motel helps. Don't tell anyone where you are, turn off your cell phones, and unplug the TV. When you get home,*

you'll find your relationship has acquired ruddy cheeks." — Dr. Ruth Westheimer, psychosexual therapist and author of *52 Lessons on Communicating Love*

In-Flight Checklist[18]

1) What does each partner in the relationship bring with them culturally and personally?
2) What were the key progressions that explain how your relationship developed, especially from "stranger" to "friendship" or to "romantic relationship"?
3) Now that you are in the relationship, what strategies do you each use to negotiate the relationship, maintain it, and resolve issues?
4) How are issues in "interracial" dating/romance/marriage the same or different from issues in "intercultural" dating/romance/marriage?

Biblical References

Acts 17:26 – *"From one man he made every nation of men that they should inhabit the whole earth; and he determined the times set for them and the exact places where they should live."*

1 Corinthians 12:12 - *"Just as a body, though one has many parts, but all its many parts form one body, so it is with Christ."*

Galatians 3:28 - *"There is neither Jew nor Gentile, neither slave nor free, nor is there male and female, for you are all one in Christ Jesus."*

Revelation 7:9 - *"... a great multitude that no one could count, from every nation, tribe, people and language, standing before the throne and before the Lamb. They were wearing white robes and were holding palm branches in their hands."*

Recommended Resources

Crohn, Joel. *Mixed Matches: How to Create Successful Interracial, Interethnic, and Interfaith Relationships*. New York: Fawcett Columbine, 1995.

Romano, Dugan. *Intercultural Marriage: Promise and Pitfalls,* 3rd ed. Boston & London: Intercultural, a Division of Nicholas Brealy, 2008.

Shelling, Grete, and J. Fraser-Smith. *In Love but Worlds Apart: Insights, Questions, and Tips for the Intercultural Couple*. Bloomington, IN: Author House, 2008.

Chapter 15

Married Again
The 2ⁿᵈ Flight, but Not Together

Pre-flight information

In the United States, researchers estimate that 40%–50% of all first marriages will end in divorce or permanent separation.[1] The risk of divorce is even higher for second marriages, about 60% within the first two years.[2]

Rebuilding a future after divorce is by no means an easy path. Some decide to remain single; others prefer to find a new partner. Dating is much more complicated the second, third, or fourth time (or more). More than 80% choose to marry again. Before you do, however, you need to be committed to a foundation of faith and an improved relationship before the "I do's" are exchanged.[3]

Do you recall how many of the Old Testament families were blended families? King David had many wives and children from them. His family demonstrates some of the hazards experienced in blended families. In 2 Samuel 13, we learn how Amnon, son of David, fell in love with Tamar, the beautiful sister of Absalom, son of David—she was Amnon's half-sister. 1 Kings 1 and 2 tell us of the jealousy between step and half-siblings. Blended families were commonplace in biblical times (usually from multiple marriages versus of death or divorce of today). Today, in America, nearly 33% of all marriages create blended families.[4]

Many couples enter into a blended remarriage with unrealistic expectations. Most tend to think the family will function much like the first marriage family had. The expectation that everyone will immediately 'get along' and love each other is a fantasy. In reality, most blended families must build the new family by first understanding the uniqueness of a blended family and its functionality.

Common Flight Rules of Blended Families

- The biological parent/child bond existed before the marriage.
- The new spouse gets an instant family upon marriage, rather than slowly through childbirth.
- Often one of the child's biological parents lives elsewhere.
- The children may have to observe visitation rights and move between homes.
- The ex-spouse will often be involved in co-parenting with one of the spouses in the new relationship.
- Some or even all of the new family members have already experienced loss through divorce or death.

"Parents have to remember and accept the fact that while they can end a marriage to someone, they will never stop being parents," said Ron Deal, speaker and author of *The Smart Stepfamily: Seven Steps to a Healthy Family*. "While you may be relieved to be out of the marriage, your children have been in a transitional crisis. How well they recover from that crisis has a lot to do with you. The key to successful co-parenting is separating the dissolution of your marriage from the parental responsibilities that remain."[5]

Marriage and Family Therapist Elizabeth Einstein, in her book, *The Stepfamily: Living, Loving, and Learning*, outlines some important remarriage preparation tips. Einstein says, "One of the most complex of family relationships is the stepfamily—a configuration resulting from remarriage with children. Its very existence is a product of death or divorce. No one forgets this; fear of its recurrence is part of the stepfamily's fragile foundation. This family faces a challenging task. Yet few people understand its special dynamics, and this lack of knowledge can lead unsuspecting stepfamilies into chaos."[6] Some experts say this grieving process can take anywhere from three to five years to complete. The death of a spouse, marriage separation, and divorce are sources of immense stress, and the grieving processes for each are similar. Yet, when divorce occurs, one must sort through emotional and economic issues with a former spouse while adjusting to a new style of parenthood.

"Any marriage is the blending of two families, not just two individuals," says Ben Silliman, family life extension specialist, University of Wyoming. We commonly bring expectations for marriage that mirror those of our 'family of origin,' watching friends and our perspectives from previous relationships. When we marry, we unite the traditions and expectations of two families: from his and from hers.

"What is important, then, is for partners to become aware of each other's expectations before going to the altar. Defining each partner's expectations is essential to the success of any marriage or couple relationship because matching behavior and expectations can be important for cooperation and satisfaction," said Silliman.

What Does the Bible Say about Christian Blended Families?

Christian blended families are becoming more and more commonplace. 1 Timothy 3:4 gives direction to men and how to manage their families well and raise children who respect the parents.   Ladies have the responsibility to teach others what is good, present herself self-controlled and pure, and then urge younger women to love their husbands and children (Titus 2:3-5). Providing for our relatives, especially those living in our household, is especially important as believers in Christ (1 Timothy 5:8). Children should be obedient to and honor their parents, the first commandment with a promise (Ephesians 6:1-3). Caring for parents and grandparents becomes the children's duty as they grow older (1 Timothy 5:4).

In prioritizing our relationship with God, If we put Him at the center of the marriage, He automatically becomes the center of the family. The first husband and wife, Adam and Eve, were created by God. He formed Eve from Adam's rib, demonstrating how men and women are to leave their parents and be joined together forever (Genesis 2:24; Matthew 19:5). A healthier marriage builds a stronger family. Parents sometimes have different thoughts on how to discipline children. However, it is vital that a consensus is reached in advance. Two families forming a blended family are coming from dissimilar households and different rules. It is crucial to establish disciplinary rules and to be consistent for all the children. Don't allow the children to stage-manage one parent against the other and don't stretch or break the rules. Always discipline the children with love and God's wisdom (Ephesians 6:4).

"We know that 60 percent of all remarriages end in divorce," said Elizabeth Einstein, nationally known stepfamily expert. "This statistic does not have to be that high. There are ways that couples can prepare for remarriage that will significantly reduce their risk of divorce."

Einstein suggests the following for couples planning to enter into a stepfamily situation:[7]

- Recognize and deal with the losses.
  - o It is important to validate losses for all of the individuals involved.
- Develop a solid couple bond.
- Make sure you have dealt with the baggage from your previous relationships so you can focus on making this relationship work. Establish clear guidelines for dealing with ex-spouses, finances, and the challenges of step parenting, including personal space for children who may not be living with your BEFORE the wedding.
- Involve the children.
  - o Be intentional about bringing both families together to get to know each other. Keep the lines of communication open with the children so they know what is going on. Some couples include their children in the wedding.
- Discuss your discipline strategy.
  - o Agreement on how discipline will take place is critical. Stepparents should take on the role of discipline with stepchildren very slowly.
- Accept continual shifts in the household.
  - o Due to the uniqueness of your new family, it will take time for people to feel secure. You must recognize that there will be some things that happen that are totally beyond your control.
- Remember, there are no ex-parents, only ex-spouses.

o No matter how strong your feelings may be about the other parent, they are still an important part of your child's life.

Pre-Flight Checklist

Many times second and third marriages present challenges not experienced in the first. Consider serious discussions on these topics and how you will navigate them before remarriage.

- Age. If you and your potential mate have a significant age gap, consider how your relationship will be impacted. Your new spouse may have children close to your age. What expectations and thoughts will they bring into the marriage? How will they be affected by having a 'step-parent' that otherwise might be a brother or sister?

- Instant Parenthood. If one, or both, of you have children from a previous marriage, consider the adjustments the children might experience. What if this marriage will bring you into parenthood for the first time?

- Past Addictions. Have either of you experienced addictions in the past? If so, discuss how the new marriage may influence those choices of past behaviors. How will you both work through a relapse?

- Anger. You each may have some underlying anxiety and anger toward your former spouse. How will you handle those challenges when presented, especially if children are involved? Have either of both of you considered completing Anger Management Counseling?

- Cultural differences. Coming from different cultures and backgrounds can create tremendous difficulties in the new relationship. A previous partner may fight for custody on the basis of not wanting the children to be exposed to different customs, religions or beliefs. Other points to consider are in chapter 14, Handling Cultural Differences – *This Radar Takes Direction-finding Awareness!*

- Medical concerns. Be intentional to discuss any medical concerns your new partner may have experienced or is currently under care. Seek the counsel of legal professionals as to surrogate decisions and life giving alternatives. Be especially cognizant of any STDs or STIs either of you have experienced.

- Jealousy. No matter how well you prepare, jealousy will arise in the new relationship. Simply the mention of your former spouse can set off feelings of resentment, bitterness, hostility and more. Consider serious discussions on how you and your new spouse plan to overcome those times when jealousy will creep in.

In-Flight Checklist

We do not suggest you look for ways to create trouble. However, discussing potential problems can be helpful. Couples should use simple brainstorming techniques to establish communication channels how they might plot a course around or through the difficult circumstances. It is okay to air any concerns and how the situations will be handled when they arise. Some common storms that may arise are:

- Negative reactions from step-children
- How to handle holidays
- Which church to attend
- Contraception
- Finances

Many remarriages are victorious and bring enormous enjoyment to the couples and families. The strength and skills of adults can reflect the stability of a remarriage, so being aware of possible problem areas helps couples to face difficult situations maturely.

Biblical References:

Nehemiah 4:14 – *"Don't be afraid of them. Remember the Lord, who is great and awesome and fight for your brothers, your sons and your daughters, your wives and your homes."*

1 Timothy 3:4 – *"He must manage his own family well and see that his children obey him, and he must do so in a manner worthy of full respect."*

Titus 2:3-5 – *"Likewise, teach the older women to be reverent in the way they live, not to be slanderers or addicted to much wine, but to teach what is good. Then they can urge the younger women to love their husbands and children, to be self-controlled and pure, to be busy at home, to be kind, and to be subject to their husbands, so that no one will malign the word of God."*

1 Timothy 5:8 – *"Anyone who does not provide for their relatives, and especially for their own household, has denied the faith and is worse than an unbeliever."*

Ephesians 6:1-3 – *"Children, obey your parents in the Lord, for this is right. "Honor your father and mother"—which is the first commandment with a promise— "so that it may go well with you and that you may enjoy long life on the earth."*

Matthew 26:38 – *"Then he said to them, "My soul is overwhelmed with sorrow to the point of death. Stay here and keep watch with me."*

Recommended Resources:

Rosberg, Gary, and Barbara Rosberg. *Divorce Proof Your Marriage.* Wheaton, IL: Tyndale House, 2004.

Marsolini, Maxine. *Blended Families; Creating Harmony as You Build a New Home Life.* Chicago: Moody, 2000.

Murphy, Jeffrey, and Charles Dettman. *The Solution for Marriages: Mentoring a New Generation.* Jupiter, FL,: Today's Promise, 2011.

Deal, Ron L. *The Smart Stepfamily*. Minneapolis, MN: Bethany House, 2006.

For more information about building strong stepfamilies go to National Stepfamily Resource Center http://stepfam.org/

Chapter 16

Trust
The Flight Succeeds With Trust!

Pre-Flight Information:

The most important element in a marriage is trust. Without trust there is no relationship or marriage. From infancy, we seek and need relationships in which we sense we are cared for, can express ourselves, and feel safe. Many people talk about trust in a relationship, but what is trust? For instance, if you don't trust your spouse, you're more likely to be irritated, worried, disheartened, mad, miserable, anxious, stressed, and more. But, if you trust your spouse, there's shared respect, more refuge, and more honesty to love, communication, and intimacy. Simply put, lack of trust is very damaging to the marriage.

Trust can always be a growth area in your marriage, regardless of how new or seasoned your marriage is. Trust is the vital component for any healthy marriage relationship! You should be intentional about creating a solid establishment of trust in your marriage; doing so will allow you to build a family that will impact generations to come!

Marriages are sanctified and need to be treated with the highest care, nurture, and love. Trust is the bond that glues marriages. Always be conscious of your actions to continually build trust, not breaking it. Broken trust in a marriage is difficult to repair.

Trust is the foundation of what makes relationships work. It is the elementary process of love and intimacy. When we lose trust, we lose safety, security, respect, love and friendship, giving in to anger, insecurity, anxiety, and fear. When distressed, we become suspicious, acting like the FBI, CIA, or police. We look through cell phones, peek at emails and question our spouse endlessly. Our lives are laced with disagreements, both grand and insignificant, and focused on what is actually taking place rather than trusting in the face value of the conversation.

In-flight Navigation Aide - *Tactical Air Navigation Aids*

1. Coming clean does work—but not completely clean.

   Lying and denial only bring more distrust, so truth along with the motivation to be responsible for your actions is the key. Details, however, can sometimes be more harmful and increase the pain. Try not to spend too much time on the details and focus on what needs to be accomplished to correct the inappropriate behavior.

2. Being defensive, righteous, or casual about the problem never works.

   Sincerity to work through the issues is important. Without genuineness, the wall will never be removed. Remove your anger (James 1:19-20), so you'll be able to 'hear' your spouse.

3. Speak of 'why' you did it.

   Sharing the struggle, a need for help, and recognizing how you arrived there will decrease the chances of future mishaps. Whatever the difficulty in your marriage (addictions, loneliness, alienation or others), take the initiative to seek Christian counseling so you may talk about your feelings, what caused the inappropriateness, and more.

4. Be an "open book."

   This means 'total transparency.' Open your cell phone, emails, internet sites and calendar. This will most likely be the most difficult exercise for you because of the secrecy you've lived in to this point. You may feel your privacy is violated or become righteous and indignant about sharing. Now is the time to ask yourself what is important: your relationship or your closed book? Once you've taken the steps to share 'everything,' you'll experience peace and relief. You'll feel as if you've taken off a 300 pound baggage from your shoulders.

5. Be aware of your spouse's need and best interests.

Begin to make choices that benefit both you and your spouse. Your needs will be met as well by simply being aware of the needs and the ability to recognize them more often. Most relationships grow healthier when a balance between meeting your needs and those of your spouse is reached. Remember, your spouse is looking at your success, ultimately leading to everyone's needs being met.

In-flight Exercises - *Traffic Situation Display.*

Renewing trust is not just a choice—it's an everyday life choice. It's about coming home to yourself and your spouse and making it work. A clear and open relationship is a valuable asset in a marriage. Lying, cheating, stealing of ourselves, and other negatives only bring a loss to what is most valued to us. Asking for help is not shameful; actually, it is admirable. If you need help, get it! If change is necessary, then do it! Establishing trust in your marriage is a big deal, so care for it that way. Trust is a very delicate, sometimes intimidating process made up of many components. A relationship can turn sour quickly if trust is not properly managed. Improperly processed, the remnants will be anger, regret and distrust. The restoring of trust is a major learning event, leading to greater love, intimacy and understanding.

The following are a few helpful exercises to restore trust.

- You come first. Seek a support group to help you manage your emotions and feelings. In her book, *The New Monogamy,* relationship expert and psychotherapist Tammy Nelson, Ph.D., suggests taking care of yourself physically as well as emotionally and recommends getting sufficient rest and practicing yoga or meditation. Concentrating on your needs is a type of self-love.

- Build on your intuition. Dr. Nelson, in her book, *The New Monogamy,* says it is necessary to work on trusting our own intuition before attempting to trust our spouse. Sometimes the sense of intuition is the greatest indicator of your partner's future honesty.

- Seek couple or group counseling. Many well trained lay counselors, and licensed professionals can walk you through the steps to rebuild trust. If you choose the group method, other couples building or repairing their marriage can be a priceless support mechanism for you both.

- What was happening in your relationship before the distrust? Do not attempt to 'blame' you or your spouse. The choice was solely his or hers and the responsibility is theirs. Making an assessment of the marriage before the event that caused the distrust can help prevent future similar experiences. Hopefully you'll be able to identify and bring resolution to the issue, giving you all the more reason to ensure success as you move forward.

- Create clearly defined understanding for accountability and dishonesty. Dishonesty cannot exist if the marriage is to succeed. Accountability is essential in building trust. A pattern of accountability will enable more trust for him or her.

- What if your spouse violates your trust again? Develop boundaries and consequences if your partner violates the sacredness of your relationship again. Have clear and concise rules each of you are committed to well in advance of another infraction. Most important, seek God's guidance and wisdom while establishing your rules.

In-flight Checklist – *Strategic Plan of Operation.*

If you would like to deepen the trust between you and your partner, please try these 10 tips:

1. What is said in the relationship stays in the relationship. One of the easiest ways to destroy trust is to tell others what your partner has shared in confidence.

2. Communicate in real time (face-to-face) with your spouse. Set aside time every day to communicate with your spouse. Don't depend on text messages, emails, and phone calls to chat

with your spouse. In person communication builds a sense of trust and security while becoming more open and vulnerable with each other.

3. What are your spouse's interests? Be considerate and do more for him or her. You'll be surprised about the reaction when your partner knows they can count on you. If he or she knows you can be counted upon to have their interests at heart, he or she will want to share more of their deepest feelings and desires with you.

4. Be sure to make good on the little promises. For example, if you say you'll pick-up the dry-cleaning, then do it! It's the small things that matter. Baby steps toward building trust leads to a strong foundation.

5. Become skilled at offering your apology when you mess up or disappoint your mate. Don't overuse, be sincere and authentic. Your spouse will be more receptive if he or she senses you are meaningful and take responsibility for your actions. Most importantly, validate and understand your partner's feelings and the impact your actions had on him or her.

6. Seek to learn more about your partner. Share deeper, personal information and history about yourself. Your goal is to find a balance on sharing. Trust is not single sided; both must be comfortable sharing with each other.

7. Leisure time is precious. You are two individuals with different likes. However, spending time together and doing things that make you each happy is important. Trust follows your willingness to experience something new that is suggested by your husband or wife. Building stronger bonds together creates more powerful trust.

8. Forgiveness is a learned experience with your husband or wife. We all get upset with one another, but learning to 'let go' as you communicate strengthens trust.

9. Spend some 'alone time' to catch up with yourself. Ask family and friends for their perspective on your relationship. You'll be surprised how beneficial the honest input can help you grow. You may gain valuable insight to help you trust your spouse even more.

10. Ride the bumps, rejoice in the dips. Our trust rises and falls as we navigate life. Look for ways you can restore confidence to your spouse that your love for him or her is greater today than when you first met.

Biblical References

Psalm 13:5 – *"But I trust in your unfailing love; my heart rejoices in your salvation."*

1 John 4:18 – *"There is no fear in love, but perfect love casts out fear. For fear has to do with punishment, and whoever fears has not been perfected in love."*

Romans 15:13 – *"May the God of hope fill you with all joy and peace in believing, so that by the power of the Holy Spirit you may abound in hope."*

Luke 16:11 – *"If then you have not been faithful in the unrighteous wealth, who will entrust to you the true riches?"*

Recommended Resources

Block, Joel D. *Broken Promises, Mended Hearts: Maintaining Trust in Love Relationships*. Lincolnwood, IL: Contemporary, 2001.

Roseberg, Gary, and Barbara Rosberg. *.Healing the Hurt in Your Marriage*. Wheaton, IL: Tyndale House, 2004.

Smalley, Gary, and Ted Cunningham. *From Anger to Intimacy: How Forgiveness Can Transform Your Marriage*. Ventura, CA: Regal, 2009.

Chapman, Gary D., and Jennifer Thomas. *The Five Languages of Apology: How to Experience Healing in All Your Relationships*.

Chicago: Northfield Pub., 2006.

Chapter 17

Marriage Expectations
The Pre-flight Experience

Pre-flight Information

Many times, during our 25 plus years of coaching engaged couples, we have asked, "What do you expect from your marriage?" only to be answered by, "I don't know." Simple as that sounds, we are saddened that most couples place more emphasis on the ceremony, living accommodations, and 'must haves' than what life together might be like. When prompted to seriously explore ideas and share with each other, many couples have difficulty defining expectations. We explore why. Again, we are dismayed as the most popular response is the lack of role models by parents, families, and friends.

Defining expectations is essential to the marriage, because a marriage is the fusion of two families, the traditions and expectations of cultures, traditions, and elements both have viewed while watching family and friends.

Dr. John Epp, author of the program *"P.I.C.K. a Partner"* (*Premarital Interpersonal Choices and Knowledge*; www.nojerks.com), suggests a strong relationship takes three things: time, talk and togetherness. These three "T's" are equally central to learning more about your prospective spouse. According to Dr. Van Epp, togetherness is where you see the person in action in many different situations—having fun, being serious, alone with you, and interacting with others. Couples begin to learn about one another when they start dating, spending time on the phone, exchanging emails, and sending text messages.

Couples with differing expectations often experience more problems in their relationship. For example, one spouse feels it's important to set aside a career and raise the children, and the other partner expects to parent while experiencing full-time employment outside the home. What about the holiday expectations and vacation to visit relatives? Some of these questions may be better answered using the tools in chapter 10, The Holidays – *Book Your Travel Plans Early* and chapter 14, Handling Cultural Differences - *This Radar Takes Direction-finding Awareness!*

When coaching couples, we often suggest using the expectations as an exercise to learn more about *active listening* and *assertive communication* methods. Great tools and definitions of active listening and assertive communication can be found in chapter 2, Communicating - *The Control Tower Is Calling.*

In-flight Navigation Aid - *Ground Delay Program*

We go through life expecting results. When you enter the grocery store, you expect the food items on your list to be in stock. While navigating the roads and highways in our community, you expect the traffic signals to function properly. When the car doesn't start, the light in the room fails to come on, or the bonus was not included in your check, you immediately feel a sense of frustration.

Instead of being constantly frustrated with your expectations, push the pause button for a few hours or even a few days. When you feel more at ease, the first question to ask yourself is where did this expectation (household chores, finances, etc.) coming from? Is it from a childhood observation? Is the expectation realistic or unrealistic? Did family and friends have an impact on your trigger point? In any case, for the relationship to be successful, compromise is essential. What may seem to be normal or obvious to you may surprise your spouse and vise versa.

In-flight Exercises - *Low Altitude Arrival/Departure Routing.*

The University of Texas suggests these steps to assist in maintaining a positive relationship:

- Tell your spouse what your needs and expectations are, keeping them within reason.

- Expect to negotiate and compromise with one another.

- Don't force your spouse to accept your expectations and you not his or hers.

- Understand and respect each other's differences, viewpoints and desires.

- Work honestly and sincerely on critical differences. Seek professional help if you come to an impasse.

- Be careful to treat your spouse with love and trust. Be sure to express your desire to work through the process.

In-flight Checklist – *Land and Hold Short Operations.*

So many times individuals confuse expectations with respect when actually they complement each other. If your expectations are met, you'll feel a sense of respect. Conversely, if you feel your spouse is respectful, then you will know many of your expectations are understood and considered. Often, we focus on what we are "getting" from our spouse, when in reality we should be concentrating on the "giving" component of respect.

A few examples are:

- Speak your words carefully. Are you intending to "punish" your mate or are you seeking more consideration? Depending on the goal, diplomacy might work better for you.

- Acknowledge contributions. Giving credit to your partner for the positive things he or she contributes will encourage trust and respect. Share your appreciation, even during moments of frustration. They'll lead to a more productive outcome in your relationship.

- Honor boundaries. Face it, we all have our "space" and don't enjoy invasion by others, including our husband or wife. Be considerate, understanding, and respectful of personal boundaries.

- Compromise. Being respected doesn't mean your needs always take priority over your partner's. Compromise provides a relationship the flexibility it needs to keep from ripping apart.

- Admit you are wrong. We all make mistakes, but admitting it takes strength. An apology should not indicate weakness or threat; it is a sign of self-confidence and self-worth.

- Earn respect. You may be in a position of honor. However, you must "earn" the respect of those around you. The position may demand honor, but you, the person, must work to gain respect as the person in that position.

- Be of character. An individual of character is much more *easily* respected. People with high levels of integrity are rarely harmful or hurtful to others.

- Show respect. To be respected, we must demonstrate respect.

When we respect others, especially our spouse, we are able to overcome the trivial-mindedness, insecurity, defenses and fear. Respecting both ourselves and our spouse builds a stronger, healthier supported marriage.

Biblical References

Mark 10:6-9 – *"But from the beginning of creation, 'God made them male and female.' 'Therefore a man shall leave his father and mother and hold fast to his wife, and the two shall become one flesh.' So they are no longer two but one flesh. What therefore God has joined together let not man separate."*

Ephesians 5:22-30 – *"Wives, submit to your own husbands, as to the Lord. For the husband is the head of the wife even as Christ is the head of the church, his body, and is himself its Savior. Now as the church* *submits to Christ, so also wives should submit in everything to their husbands.*

Husbands, love your wives, as Christ loved the church and gave himself up for her, that he might sanctify her, having cleansed her by the washing of water with the word, so that he might present the church to himself in splendor, without spot or wrinkle or any such thing, that she might be holy and without blemish. In the same way husbands should love their wives as their own bodies. He who loves his wife loves himself. For no one ever hated his own flesh, but nourishes and cherishes it, just as Christ does the church, because we are members of his body."

Recommended Resources

Larson, Jeffrey H. *Should We Stay Together: The Compatibility Test.* San Francisco, CA: Jossey-Bass, 2000.

Chapter 18

Navigational Cards
The Checkpoints along the Journey

A premium resource, our Navigational Cards, can be obtained in the Resources section of *The Marriage Journey* website.

The cards serve as navigation "checkpoints" similar to most flight requirements to report their route checkpoints with flight control centers! Each deck of cards contains 54 words relative to marriage, one on every card. Each word is supported by a scripture for that word. That word is intended to provoke discussion, thought and strength to the couple. The Navigation Cards help couples to learn where they are aligned and reveal strength in their marriage. At other times, they'll discover a word that prompts an opportunity for growth. (We call it flight path adjustment.) Together, the couple can experience joy and a better understanding of their spouse by using a simple set of cards (flight guides).

How are the cards important in your discussion? Begin by selecting twelve (12) cards that contain significant words to you on today's discussion. Once you both have selected your cards, share the results, noting any similar words. Set the cards with similar words aside for now.

Now share why you chose the words (cards), using the Assertive Communication and Active Listening skills you learned in chapter 2, Communicating - *The Control Tower Is Calling* and chapter 17, Marriage Expectations - *The Pre-flight Experience*. Be sure to read and share the corresponding Scripture on each of these cards, and then tell your partner how that Scripture relates to the discussion today.

Sort the cards again, including the cards with similar words, narrowing your selection to six cards. Compare your selection with your spouse again. Once again, set aside any cards with similar words. Explore, once again, why these cards continue to be important to you in this conversation. (Don't use the same description you used above, because the reason you chose these cards have a deeper meaning to you now than a few minutes before.)

Gather your cards together one more time, including the ones you set aside. Sort them again, but this time, select the single most significant word to you. Now compare this sorting result with your spouse's choice. Did you select a card with the same word or have you each chosen a unique card? These cards, and the Scriptures, are the most meaningful in your relationship at this moment. Read the verse to each other, share the word, and then discuss why you chose this single card. Speak with sincerity and love. Be sure you are not talking with a tone of aggression, distrust, or disbelief. Be positive, choose kind phrases.

Remember, the discussion and choices will differ, because the topic of discussion is never the same. (Even if the subject is similar, the discussion will change because the elements leading to the dialogue differ.) The words and Scripture for each conversation will be unique to that exchange and have a special impact on your result.

Use the cards often, in many scenarios, to help you gain a better understanding of your spouse and yourself. Combine them with the Conflict Resolution steps, Forgiveness discussions, Stress Management techniques and more.

Additional resources, updates and downloadable material is available from www.themarriage-journey/resources

State Marriage Handbooks (USA)

Several states have published marriage handbooks as a free public resource. Some of these are well done while others are lacking in scope, content, and/or time-tested values.

This list is provided as a resource to our readers, and is not specifically endorsed by us. Feel free to use these as you see fit since they were developed through public financing and are in the public domain.

See the Resources section of TheMarriage-Journey.com for periodic updates to this list.

Alabama

aces.edu/pubs/docs/H/HE-0829/HE-0829.pdf

The handbook includes information about money, balancing work and family, responsibilities in the home, children, and in-laws. The resource also addresses substance abuse, gambling, mental health problems, sexual infidelity, and other issues that hurt relationships.

Colorado

smartmarriages.org/colorado.handbook.html

Apparently no longer being produced and distributed, this handbook included information on communication skills, dealing with conflict, and understanding expectations.

Florida

flclerks.com/PDF/2000_2001_pdfs/7-99_VERSION_Family_Law_Handbook.pdf

The *Family/Marriage Law Handbook* is required by the State of Florida to be read by all marriage license applicants before the marriage license is issued.

Louisiana

dss.state.la.us/assets/docs/searchable/OFS/GuideMarriageChild/Marriage Matters.pdf

This graphically appealing handbook offers creative pop quiz exercises for couples. It includes information about handling conflict and techniques for developing listening skills.

Oklahoma

marriageok.net/MarriageOKMagazine.pdf

This handbook has extensive information about marriage license requirements, benefits of a healthy marriage, special issues with marrying young, conflict resolution, and parenting skills.

Texas

oag.state.tx.us/AG_Publications/pdfs/marriage.pdf

This handbook offers a workbook style interaction with couples and addresses personality differences, conflict issues, communication skills, children, money, and faith issues.

Utah

extension.usu.edu/files/publications/publication/Marriage_2007.pdf

Based on the Alabama handbook as a model, this resource provides basic tips for managing relational expectations, discussing shared goals, and handling issues related to finances, parenting, in-laws, and remarriage.

.

End Notes

Chapter 01: Our Union With Christ - *God Is The Pilot, We Are the Co-pilots*

1. Stoop, Jan, and David A. Stoop. *When Couples Pray Together: Creating Intimacy and Spiritual Wholeness*. Ann Arbor, MI: Vine, 2000. 9.

2. Price, Rev. Bill. "Bible Prayer Fellowship - About Us." *Bible Prayer Fellowship - Teaching United Prayer*. Bible Prayer Fellowship - Teaching United Prayer, 2011. praywithchrist.org/aboutus.php.

3. Burns, Jim. "Grow Towards Spiritual Intimacy in Your Marriage." *Grow Towards Spiritual Intimacy in Your Marriage*. Crosswalk.com, 26 July 2007. Web. 15 Jan. 2014. http://www.crosswalk.com/family/marriage/grow-towards-spiritual-intimacy-in-your-marriage-1407864.html.

Chapter 02: Communicating – *The Control Tower is Calling*

1. For more on the Imago Dialogue, go to gettingtheloveyouwant.com/articles/imago-dialogue-101

2. Adapted from Murphy, Jeff and Dettman, Chuck, The Solution for Marriages, CreateSpace, Jupiter, FL, 2011, Pg. 51.

3. Ibid.

4. Olson, David H. L., and Amy K. Olson. *Empowering Couples: Building on Your Strengths*. Minneapolis, MN: Life Innovations, 2000. Pg. 31.

Chapter 03: Managing and Coping With Stress - *Make Your Flight Smooth*

1. Peter J. Larsen, Ph.D., and David H. Olsen, Ph.D., Popadic, Tim, MFT, *Couple Checkup & Date Nights @ Chick-fil-A*. A Community Based Marriage Enrichment Campaign. Roseville,

MN: Life Innovations, 2011. *Couple Checkup & Date Nights @ Chick-fil-A*. Chick-fil-A, Couple Check-up, Marriage Alive, 1 June 2011. Web. 14 Nov. 2013.

2. Holmes TH, Rahe RH (1967). "The Social Readjustment Rating Scale". J Psychosom Res 11 (2): 213–8. Commonly known as the Holmes and Rahe Stress Scale. Adapted by authors.

Chapter 04: Resolving Conflict - *Navigating Turbulence*

1. Gottman, John Mordechai, and Nan Silver. *The Seven Principles for Making Marriage Work*. New York: Three Rivers, 1999.27

2. Scott Stanley and others, *A Lasting Promise: A Christian Guide to Fighting for Your Marriage*, (San Francisco: Jossey-Bass, 1998), 115-137.

3. Gottman, John, and Nan Silver. *The Seven Principles for Making Marriage Work*. New York, NY: Three Rivers, 1999.27

4. Gottman, John, and Nan Silver. *The Seven Principles for Making Marriage Work*. New York, NY: Three Rivers, 1999.40

Chapter 05: Granting Forgiveness - *Let God Navigate Your Heart*

1. Sande, Ken. *The Peacemaker: A Biblical Guide to Resolving Personal Conflict*. 3rd ed. Grand Rapids, MI: Baker, 1997. Sixth Printing, October 2006.

2. Ibid.

3. (2010-04-01). The New Oxford American Dictionary (Kindle Locations 168792 and 424149-424150). Oxford University Press. Kindle Edition.

Chapter 06 : Managing God's Money

1. "Life of Hudson Taylor, Founder of the China Inland Mission." *Life of Hudson Taylor, Founder of the China Inland Mission*. Truthnet.org, n.d. Web. 11 Aug. 2013.

http://www.truthnet.org/Christianity/biography/HudsonTaylor/Chapter3.htm

2. Blue, Ron, and Jeremy White. *Faith-based Family Finances*. Carol Stream, IL: Tyndale House, 2008.

3. Ramsey, Dave. "Marriage-Risking Money Secrets." CBS News, The Early Show. *CBSNews*. CBS Interactive, 22 Apr. 2009. Web. 11 Aug. 2013. http://www.cbsnews.com/stories/2008/02/12/earlyshow/contributors/daveramsey/main3820349.shtml.

4. Rockefeller, Sr., John D. *Give Him the First Part*. Campus Crusade for Christ International, 25 May 2011. ccci.org/training-and-growth/devotional-life/todays-promise/tp0525.htm.

Chapter 07: The Internet, Social Media, and Friends - *Protecting Your Intercontinental Flight Path*

1. "Big Surge in Social Networking Evidence Says Survey of Nation's Top Divorce Lawyers." *AAML National*. American Academy of Matrimonial Lawyers, 10 Feb. 2010. Web. 23 Aug. 2013. http://www.aaml.org/about-the-academy/press/press-releases/e-discovery/big-surge-social-networking-evidence-says-survey-

2. Blue, Ron, and Jeremy White. *Faith-based Family Finances*. Carol Stream, IL: Tyndale House, 2008.

3. Mogal, Rich. "Protect Your Privacy: Take Control of Social Networking." *Macworld*. MacWorld.com, 23 Feb. 2011. Web. 23 Aug. 2013. http://www.macworld.com/article/1158122/protect_privacy_social_networks.html

Chapter 08: How Cohabitation Impacts the Flight Plan

1. VanGoethem, Jeff. *Living Together: a Guide to Counseling Unmarried Couples*. Grand Rapids, MI: Kregel Academic & Professional, 2005. 105.

2. Jason, Sharon. "Cohabiting Has Little Effect on Marriage Success." USA Today. USA Today, 14 Oct. 2010. Usatoday.com/news/health/2010-03-02-cohabiting02_N.htm

3. Binstock, Georgina, and Arland Thornton. "Separations, Reconciliations, and Living Apart in Cohabiting and Marital Unions." *Journal of Marriage and Family* 65.2 (2003): 432-43.

4. Hill, PhD, John R., and Sharon G. Evans, MA. "Effects of Cohabitation Length on Personal and Relational Well Being." Alabama Policy Institute, 3 Aug. 2006. Alabamapolicy.org/pdf/cohabitation.pdf.

5. Bennett, Neil G., Ann Klimas Blanc, and David E. Bloom. "Commitment and the Modern Union: Assessing the Link between Premarital Cohabitation and Subsequent Marital Stability." *American Sociological Review* 53.1 (1988): 127-38. jstor.org/pss/2095738; T. K. Burch & A. K. Madan, Union Formation and Dissolution: Results from the 1984 Family History Survey (Ottawa: Statistics Canada, Catalogue No. 99-963) (1986); Catherine Cohan & Stacey Kleinbaum, "Toward a greater understanding of the cohabitation effect: Premarital cohabitation and marital communication." *Journal of Marriage and the Family* 64 (2002): 180-192; D. M. Fergusson, L. J. Horwood, & F. T. Shannon, "A proportional hazards model of family breakdown." *Journal of Marriage and the Family* 46 (1984) 539-549; and Zheng Wu, "Premarital cohabitation and post marital cohabiting union formation." *Journal of Family Issues* 16 (1995) 212-232.

6. Susan L. Brown, "Union Transitions Among Cohabiters: The Significance of Relationship Assessment and Expectations." *Journal of Marriage and the Family* 62 (2000): 833-846.

7. McManus, Michael J., and Harriett McManus. Introduction. *Living Together: Myths, Risks & Answers*. New York: Howard, 2008. 60-61.

8. Hall, David R., and John Z. Zhoa. "Cohabitation and Divorce in Canada." *Journal of Marriage and the Family* May (1995): 421-27.

9. Stanley, Scott. *The Power of Commitment: a Guide to Active, Lifelong Love*. San Francisco: Jossey-Bass, 2005. 152.

10. Hill, PhD, John R., and Sharon G. Evans, MA. "Effects of Cohabitation Length on Personal and Relational Well Being." Alabama Policy Institute, 3 Aug. 2006. 12.

12. All About Cohabitating Before Marriage, Psychological Reasons, members.aol.com/cohabiting/index.htm July 1999

13. Hill, PhD, John R., and Sharon G. Evans, MA. "Effects of Cohabitation Length on Personal and Relational Well Being." Alabama Policy Institute, 3 Aug. 2006. 3.

14. McManus, Michael J. *Marriage Savers: Helping Your Friends and Family Stay Married*. Grand Rapids, MI: Zondervan Pub. House, 1993.

15. Gordon, Serena. ""Marriage" - Jim L. Wilson." *Sermons.Logos.com*. Fresh Ministry, Jan. 2009. sermons.logos.com/submissions/80537-Marriage.

16. Catherine Cohan & Stacey Kleinbaum, "Toward a greater understanding of the cohabitation effect: Premarital cohabitation and marital communication." *Journal of Marriage and the Family* 64 (2002): 180-192.

17. DeMaris, A., and G. R. Leslie. "Cohabitation with Future Spouse: Its Influence upon Marital Satisfaction and Communication." *Journal of Marriage and Family* 46 (1984): 77-84.

18. Stafford, Laura, Susan L. Klein, and Caroline T. Rankin. "Married Individuals, Cohabiters, and Cohabiters Who Marry: A Longitudinal Study of Relational and Individual Well-Being." *Journal of Social and Personal Relationships* April.21 (2004): 231-48.

19. Dush, Claire M. Kamp, Catherine L. Cohan, and Paul R. Amato. "The Relationship Between Cohabitation and Marital Quality and Stability: Change Across Cohorts?" *Journal of Marriage and Family* 65.3 (2003): 539-49.

20. Stanley, S. M., S. W. Whitton, and H. J. Markman. "Maybe I Do: Interpersonal Commitment and Premarital or Non-marital Cohabitation." *Journal of Family Issues* 25 (2004): 496-519.

21. Harley, Jr., Ph.D, William F. "Meet Dr. Harley." *Marriage Builders ® - Successful Marriage Advice*. Marriage Builders ®. 27 June 2011.. marriagebuilders.com/graphic/mbi2000_meet.html.

22. DeMaris, Alfred, and William MacDonald. "Premarital Cohabitation and Marital Instability: A Test of the Unconventionality Hypothesis." *Journal of Marriage and the Family* 55 (1993): 399-407.

23. Downridge, Douglas A., and Silvia S. Halli. "'Living in Sin' and Sinful Living: Toward Filling a Gap in the Explanation of Violence against Women." *Aggression and Violent Behavior* November-December 5.6 (2000): 565-83. *Science Direct*. Science Direct, 16 Nov. 2000. sciencedirect.com/science/article/pii/S1359178999000038.

24. McManus, Mike. "Articles: Better Together? Only in Holy Matrimony, Not in Cohabitation." *Marriage Resources for Clergy @ Marriageresourcesforclergy.com*. Marriage Resources for Clergy, 13 Mar. 2008. .marriageresourcesforclergy.com/site/Articles/articles017.htm.

25. Brown, S., and A. Booth. "Cohabitation versus Marriage: A Comparison of Relationship Quality." *Journal of Marriage and Family* 58 (1996): 667-68.

26. Catherine Cohan & Stacey Kleinbaum, "Toward a greater understanding of the cohabitation effect: Premarital cohabitation and marital communication." *Journal of Marriage and the Family* 64 (2002): 180-192. doi: 10.1111/j.1741-3737.2002.00180.x

27. VanGoethem, Jeff. *Living Together: a Guide to Counseling Unmarried Couples.* Grand Rapids, MI: Kregel Academic & Professional, 2005. 48-49.

28. Wilcox, Ph.D, W. Bradford. "Why the Ring Matters." *New York Times* [New York] 20 Dec. 2010. nytimes.com/roomfordebate/2010/12/19/why-remarry/why-the-ring-mattershusbandsanddads.com

Chapter 10: The Holidays – *Book Your Travel Plans Early*

1. Shern, David, Ph.D. "Survey Identifies Top Holiday Stressors, Who's Most Stressed." *: Mental Health America.* Mental Health America, 7 Dec. 2006. Web. 12 June 2013. http://www.mentalhealthamerica.net/index.cfm?objectid=0F7D2 087-1372-4D20-C8469F6166842DE3.

2. Murphy, Jeffrey, and Charles Dettman. *The Solution for Marriages: Mentoring a New Generation.* Jupiter, FL,: Today's Promise, 2011.

Chapter 12: Joy and Sorrow

1. Young, William P. *The Shack: Reflections for Every Day of the Year.* Newbury Park, CA: Windblown Media, 2012.

2. Wilson, Scott. "Word." *Sermons.HillsongKonstanz.* Hillsong Germany, 27 Mar. 2011. Web. 12 Sept. 2013. http://sermons.hillsongkonstanz.de/11_03_27_SW-am.mp3.

3. Knaack, Kerstin. "Wellness Wednesday: Why Hide? My Journey of Hope, Faith and Overcoming." *SheLoves Magazine.* SheLovesMagazine.com, 15 Feb. 2012. Web. 12 Sept. 2013. http://shelovesmagazine.com/2012/wellness-wednesday-why-hide-my-journey-of-hope-faith-and-overcoming/.

Chapter 13 Intimacy In Marriage - *Enjoy the Flight God's Way*

1. *Sex, A Study of the Good Bits of Song of Solomon.* By Mark Driscoll. Edinburgh, Scotland. Presentation.

2. Gordon, Jim & Carrie, and Josh & Sarah Gordon. "The Intimate Couple - Igniting Passion in the Marriage of Your Dreams!" *The Intimate Couple, Igniting Passion in the Marriage of Your Dreams!* http://www.the-intimate-couple.com/, 2007. Web. 18 Sept. 2013. http://www.the-intimate-couple.com.

Chapter 14: Handling Cultural Differences - *This Radar Takes Direction-finding Awareness!*

1. In this chapter, "cultural" is broadly used to include race, religion, country of origin, etc.

2. Pew Forum on Religion & Public Life, Pew Research Center, and Pew Forum Web Publishing and Communications. "Summary of Key Findings." *Statistics on Religion in America Report.* Pew Research Center's Religion & Public Life Project, Feb. 2008. Web. 14 Nov. 2013. http://religions.pewforum.org/reports/.

3. Kreider, Rose M. "A Look at Interracial and Interethnic Married Couple Households in the U.S. in 2010." *A Look at Interracial and Interethnic Married Couple Households in the U.S. in 2010.* U.S. Cesnus Bureau, 26 Apr. 2012. Web. 14 Nov. 2013. http://blogs.census.gov/2012/04/26/a-look-at-interracial-and-interethnic-married-couple-households-in-the-u-s-in-2010/.

4. Chen, J., & Takeuchi, D. T. (2011). Intermarriage, ethnic identity, and perceived social standing among Asian women in the United

States. *Journal of Marriage and Family, 73,* 876–888.

5. McCarthy, K. (2007). Pluralist family values: Domestic strategies for living with religious difference. *The Annals of the American Academy of Political and Social Science, 612,* 188–208.

6. Kalmijn, M., & Van Tubergen, F. (2010). A comparative perspective on intermarriage: Explaining differences among national-origin groups in the United States. *Demography, 47*(2), 459–479.

7. Quin, Z., & Lichter, D. (2011). Changing patterns of inter- racial marriage in a multiracial society. *Journal of Marriage and Family, 73,* 1065–1084.

8. See note 4 above.

9. Seshadri, G., and Knudson-Martin, C. (2012). How couples manage interracial and intercultural differences: Implications for clinical practice. *Journal of Marital and Family Therapy.* Doi: 10.1111/j.1752-0606.2011.00262.x

10. Bustamante, R. M., Nelson, J. A., Henricksen Jr., R. C., & Monakes, S. (2011). Intercultural couples: Coping with culture-related stressors. *The Family Journal: Counseling and Therapy for Couples and Families, 19*(2), 154–164.

11. Heaton, T. B. (2002). Factors contributing to increasing marital stability in the United States. *Journal of Family Issues, 23,* 392–409.

12. Bratter, J. L., & Eschbach, K. (2006). "What about the couple?" Interracial marriage and psychological distress. *Social Sciences Research, 35,* 1025–1047.

13. Bratter, J. L., & King, R. B. (2008). "But will it last?": Marital instability among interracial and same-race couples. *Family Relations, 57,* 160–171.

14. See note 12 above.

15. Zhang, Y., & Van Hook, J. (2009). Marital dissolution among interracial couples. *Journal of Marriage and Family, 71,* 95–107.

16. Inman, A. G., Altman, A., Kaduvettoor-Davidson, A., Carr, A., & Walker, J. A. (2011). Cultural intersections: A qualitative inquiry into the experience of Asian Indian- White interracial couples. *Family Process, 50*(2), 248–266.

17. Burleigh, Nina. "5 Best Things to Do for Your Relationship - Oprah.com." *Oprah.com*. The Oprah Magazine, May 2005. Web. 14 Nov. 2013. http://www.oprah.com/relationships/5-Best-Things-to-Do-for-Your-Relationship#ixzz2kSToRf00.

18. Baldwin, John R. "Communication 372 – Theory and Research in Intercultural Communication." *Communication in Intercultural Relationships*. Illinois State University - School of Communication, 6 June 2011. Web. 14 Nov. 2013. http://my.ilstu.edu/~jrbaldw/372/ICRelationships.htm.

Chapter 15: Married Again. *The 2ⁿᵈ Flight, but Not Together*

1. Hawkins, Alan J., Ph.D., and Tamara A. Fackrell, J.D. "Lesson 3 - How Common Is Divorce and What Are the Reasons?" *Lesson 3 - How Common Is Divorce and What Are the Reasons?* Utah State University, Oct. 2009. Web. 14 Nov. 2013. http://divorce.usu.edu/htm/lesson-3.

2. Popenoe, D., & Whitehead, B. D. (2007). The state of our unions 2007: The social health of marriage in America. Piscataway, NJ: The National Marriage Project. (See pp. 18–19.)

3. Bramlett, M. D., & Mosher, W. D. (2002). Cohabitation, marriage, divorce, and remarriage in the United States. Vital and Health Statistics, 23(22). Hyattsville, MD: National Center for Health Statistics.

4. Peter J. Larsen, Ph.D., and David H. Olsen, Ph.D., Popadic, Tim, MFT, *Couple Checkup & Date Nights @ Chick-fil-A*. A Community Based Marriage Enrichment Campaign. Roseville,

MN: Life Innovations, 2011. *Couple Checkup & Date Nights @ Chick-fil-A.* Chick-fil-A, Couple Check-up, Marriage Alive, 1 June 2011. Web. 14 Nov. 2013.

5. Deal, Ron L. *Smart Stepfamily, The: Seven Steps to a Healthy Family.* Reprinted ed. Minneapolis, MN: Bethany House, 2006.

6. Einstein, Elizabeth. *The Stepfamily: Living, Loving, and Learning.* New York: Macmillan, 1988.

7. "Building Strong Stepfamilies." *Building Strong Stepfamilies.* First Things First, Oct. 2013. Web. 11 Nov. 2013. http://firstthings.org/building-strong-stepfamilies.

About the Authors

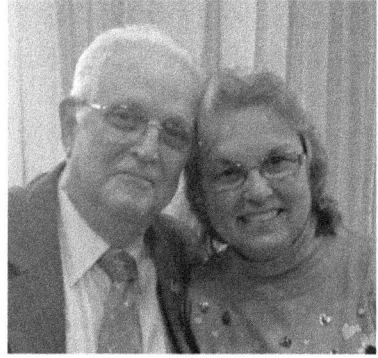

Mae and Chuck met in 7th grade, dated in High School, and married in 1969, just prior to Chuck's Vietnam tour.

They began mentoring in home Bible studies and saw how their Christ-centered relationship was "different" from others. Though far from "perfect," their marriage and commitment to Christ demonstrated a peace and happiness that intrigued other couples. This became the opportunity to mentor other couples and to teach them to *work* at their relationship and *grow* their *love* for one another (with Christ) each day.

Chuck and Mae have two adult children, Glynn and Barbara, and seven grandchildren.

Executive Director and Founder of Today's Promise, Inc., Chuck is an ordained minister with more than 12-years in couple and professional life-coaching experience. Chuck is known as a premier marriage, relationship, budget and career coaching mentor throughout the nation—having been recognized by the NY Times, CBS Evening News, and the Harvard School of Business, among others. Chuck holds a Bachelor of Science in Business and Finance from Barry University, graduating cum laude. He was formerly employed by the U.S. Under Secretary of the Treasury in local banks as a loan officer, Junior Vice President, and auditor which provided unprecedented exposure to the financial industry.

He holds many certifications, including a former Florida State Teaching Certificate as an Occupational Therapist for Secondary Education and a Certified Crown Financial Budget Coach/Counselor. He is a Certified Marriage Mentor for PREPARE/ENRICH marriage preparation, and he coaches those already married. He holds certification as a Seminar Director for PREPARE/ENRICH, providing training to clergy, professional counselors, and mentor couples. He proudly serves as a 15th Judicial Circuit Court Registered Provider for marriage education, qualifying couples for discounted marriage licensure. He is a Master

Instructor for START SMART, a premarital training course that teaches specific skills to seriously dating or engaged couples. An instructor for PICK a Partner, also known as *"How to Avoid Marrying a Jerk(ette),"* a class that instructs unmarried individuals in how to best prepare for future committed relationships.

Chuck co-authored *The Solution for Marriages;* dedicated tips to marriage mentors proven to be successful in helping others build the foundation for life-long, satisfying marriages.

Now, *The Marriage Journey, A Flight Plan to Your Healthy Marriage,* provides the flight plan for marriages to rely on, not if, but when they face the turbulence experienced by every couple. It contains powerful, faith-based references used by the authors in their own 45 plus years of marriage.

www.ingramcontent.com/pod-product-compliance
Lightning Source LLC
LaVergne TN
LVHW011157080426
835508LV00007B/450